Sylvie Vallee

Touch

of Nature to

Abundance

How to attract money and all your dreams.

An inspiring guide of spiritual ideas and tools that will change your life and your financial situation beyond your expectations

Editor: Sylvie Vallée
Cover design: lpublicidades.com
First printing: 2011
Legal deposit 2011

Vallée, Sylvie, 1963

Touch of nature to abundance:
How to attract money and all your dreams

Translation of: L'abondance par la nature:
Comment attirer l'argent et tous vos rêves

Includes bibliographical references.

ISBN 978-2-924035-03-0
Original edition ISBN 978-9-924035-00-9

1. Success - Psychological Aspects. 2. Wealth.
3.Change (Psychology).

I. Title

BF637.S8V3413 2011   158.1   C2011-942065-1

www. abundancethrunature.com

In these pages, you will learn
simple techniques that will allow
you to attract everything you desire.
The Law of Attraction is simplified and the
ideas presented will inspire families
to understand how to attract their dreams
by enhancing their thoughts, words,
emotions and vibrations,
while having fun doing it.

Table of content

My sincere thanks

To nature, which is so dear to me, and which has allowed me to grow through its beauty and abundance. Also, to horses and dogs, which gave me valuable lessons that allowed me to get in touch with my true nature.

To our riding school, for the inspiration it gave me to bring our teaching to a whole new level. I have had the privilege of witnessing many positive transformations and I and our team are grateful to have contributed to them.

To Joe Vitale, Rhonda Byrne, Jack Candfield, Anthony Robbins and many others for their books and tools about personal growth, which have allowed me to understand many of the concepts that led to my personal growth more quickly.

To Peak Potential for their teaching about the concept of a rich and open spirit, as well as on financial management.

To Total Blueprint for their quality training that has stimulated me to share my message.

To all those I have had the privilege of working with in my life and who have contributed to making me a better person, able to travel on a more empowering and fulfilling life.

The biggest THANK YOU to my family.

To my parents, for their education and the values they passed on to me, which are the foundations of my teaching.

To my wonderful husband, Sylvain, who has let me grow and create my personal growth material, without always understanding. He always gives me his unconditional support.

To my five beloved, passionate daughters Vanessa, Kaïla, Mandy Rose-Marie and Megan, who have been my inspiration. Through their joy, their energy, their goodness and their dreams they have motivated me to always excel and to help others do the same.

Preface

Your road to happiness,
abundance, wealth and health
reveals itself to you naturally.
Sylvie Vallée

*W*elcome and congratulations!

I congratulate you for making the decision to come along on the path that will lead you to all the best that you can imagine for yourself and that is destined for you. You deserve it!

If you have not experienced success or happiness, perhaps it is simply because you have not yet discovered the secret to getting them. Do you feel that, in spite of all your efforts to reach your dreams for a better life, you are just treading water in terms of results?

The secret is simple. It is simply a universal law, the Law of Attraction. This law states that "What we focus our attention on, we bring into our lives."

This Law of Attraction is activated in many ways. We can all personalize our attracting powers. I have developed a methodology that has allowed me to attract miracles. Thru the following chapters, I reveal the details of this methodology. You will understand how

3

you can also apply these ten steps of my "Touch of Nature" Creation Process to attract what you desire. It is absolutely easy and fun and you will quickly see results.

YOU CREATE
WHATEVER YOU FOCUS
YOUR THOUGHTS ON.

If your thoughts are constantly focused on lack of money, illness, or your unhappiness, then that's exactly what you attract into your life.

If on the other hand, your thoughts are directed towards abundance, happiness, health and prosperity, that is what you will bring in your life. Isn't that much better? However, it is difficult to focus our attention on what we do not have. Unconscious thoughts can also prevent us from attaining what we desire. Later on, we will discuss this subject more thoroughly.

The good news is that we can learn to set our focus on what we want to attract into our lives.

You do not need anything to succeed. Anyone can do it, even children. You simply need to condition your mind through various simple methods.

My life has been completely transformed beyond my expectations, once I applied specific steps and used simple and easy tools.

I am no different than you. I have experienced lots of trials, difficulties and financial problems. My path has been an intense quest for happiness and abundance. Like many of you, I have read countless numbers of books, attended many seminars and bought many different products. But I was always trying to fill this emptiness inside which would allow me to flourish.

I have had challenging experiences where I have applied certain principles in an intuitive manner. I obtained results that were so much more extraordinary than I could have imagined. I have then developed an interest, learned and experimented many concepts and products related to personal growth.

My personal experiences and my passion for everything related to happiness, abundance, wealth, love and health have allowed me to develop techniques that have completely transformed my life, the life of my family and many other families.

Everyone can use this amazing material, even children. It is also very important to give access to this information to families and children. They are the seed of our society. By sharing the tools proposed in this book, it is a better world that you are contributing to create for yourself and your loved ones. You become the pioneers of this new movement allowing everyone to connect to their source and their creative power thru nature.

By modifying our beliefs about our life conception and our creative powers, we discover an access to a universe of possibilities. Nature is so energizing and we can all use it to enhance our life.

Our world is in evolution and we are now in the ideal moment to make adjustments that have the power to transform our reality.

Many have already proved that we can create our reality. We all have creative powers. We must now learn how to articulate them so that we can attract all our dreams. The "Touch of Nature" Creation Process that I am sharing with you has transformed my life, the life of entire families and many others.

It is now your turn to discover it and attract magic into your life. It is your turn to realize how much fun it is to grow and see yourself blossom as well.

Chapter 1

Introduction

*W*hat do you desire?

Do you want to attract happiness, health, abundance, wealth, love, joy, peace? All your desires are allowed.

For some, happiness is to be free, while for others it is simply to be with those they love and to share good times together.

Some may seek good health. And of course, the interpretation of health is different for everyone. But we all aspire to fully enjoy life in a body that allows us to do what we want.

For many, abundance, money or anything that this allows them to obtain, arouse an interest. You all have different dreams and you can achieve them!

Now, more than ever, it is the best time to realign yourself on your thru potential.

We all realize that our actual way of living has created a frail world. Our economy is not flourishing and families are experiencing separations more than ever. Most of the population is losing goods that took a lifetime to acquire, people are consuming drugs and medication in increasing amounts... In short, too many people are unhappy. Most of them are looking for happiness in material goods or immediate pleasures. We must now understand that our world could be much better and that we have the power to create this better world.

Even if the door that gives access to happiness does not require a key to open it, many people are not willing to turn this doorknob that gives access to happiness and a better life.

Quantum physics have proven thru many experiences, that we can change our reality, by modifying our thoughts, words and vibrations.

Technology also gives us access to a diversity of tools and information that opens the path to multiple possibilities.

This book is filled with easy and inspiring tools that have the power to transform your life as they have done for myself and for many other individuals and families. The approach I propose is fun, simple and powerful. Results may appear more quickly than you would have thought. You are going to discover many of my personal secrets. I will guide you up to the last page of this book. Use this material as often as you wish.

The creation process that I use with a lot of success is presented and detailed in the following chapters.

Here is the **"Touch of Nature" Creation Process** that you will discover:

1) Be grateful for everything that is beautiful and good.

2) State what you no longer want.

3) Define what you do want.
   (I want – Why?)

4) Outline your intention (your desire) and put it in writing.

5) Formulate affirmations that support your intentions (desires).

6) Believe with certainty that it is possible.

7) Visualize your life with your intentions realized.

8) Act as if your intention has already been realized.

9) Take action to achieve your intentions (desires).

10) Detach yourself from outcomes, let go.

While going thru the chapters of this book, you will understand why many become abundance magnets, attracting all what they desire, while some others push all the good things away from them.

Some of the proposed steps may require some efforts on your part. However, I will try to help you out by offering tricks and examples.

You can all succeed while letting yourself be inspired thru nature and by having fun attracting your dreams. If I have been able to do this, and if many others and whole families have transformed their life, then you can do it too.

I would like to help you access a better life thru shortcuts and thru our inspiring material. You will be able to spare many years of unpleasant experiences and doubt. Wish I would have had access to this kind of helpful material many years before.

The secrets and the steps revealed in this book are based on my research, my experiences and my successes. Before structuring them, I made many mistakes and had many unpleasant experiences that I would like you to avoid. I worked so hard that at one point, I endangered my health. I was feeling pushed in every direction and unpleasant experiences kept coming one after the other. I know that many of you have lived through similar experiences. I certainly know perfectly how terrible this feels and how we are seeking the sun to shine in our life. I have found it, and would like to share this journey with you, so that you can get your results to appear more quickly.

A friend once said to me, that if I wanted to make a better world, first I had to be a better person. This would contribute to the improvement of our world. I would sincerely love that, together, we all become better persons, releasing our true potential and learning how to attract everything we want for the greater good of all.

TO HELP ACHIEVE
A BETTER WORLD,
YOU SIMPLY NEED TO BECOME
A BETTER PERSON.

This book is not only a practical guide, it is my story.

I don't pretend to know everything, but I would like to share with you what I have learned and experienced and what has worked in my life. If it can inspire you and help you, I'll feel fulfilled. I always learn and evolve, just as you do. I constantly discover new methods that allow me to attract what I desire into my life. I have realized that our power of attraction increases considerably when we radiate a lot of love. This is why the Law of Attraction is also called the Law of Love.

I will reveal to you, periods in my life when I experienced events that were very difficult to bear. However, the most difficult were also the most rewarding on a spiritual level. They have allowed me to grow and find internal strength that I didn't know I had.

I learned a life lesson: To move forward and continue growing, we must focus our attention on solutions. One must not just moan and complain. In other words, you must simply learn to think in new ways, focusing attention on the things you love, for which you feel love. It's a way of thinking completely differently and constructively from the way we've been conditioned to think.

You can now rejoice in seeing your life filled with everything that you aspire to: happiness, health, abundance, wealth, love, joy, peace. You are about to draw these things to you and create the life you've dreamed of.

☯ Recommended Actions

Rejoice, your dreams are becoming closer.
Visit our website
www.abundancethrunature.com
you will find free material.

Chapter 2

My story, the beginning of my transformation

*T*oday, I am happy and Oh, so grateful!

My life has improved so much during these last years. I'm not trying to be pretentious, but I'd like you to understand that change can happen so quickly and in ways that are so much more positive than we can imagine.

How thankful I am!

My family and I live a dream life and it gets better all the time. Together, we apply the "Touch of Nature" Creation Process. For my part, I appreciate nature that gives me inspiration and I do what enthralls me most, and that is, helping families becoming magnets attracting their dreams. Our daughters are following their respective passions and we're here, Sylvain and I, to support them in achieving their dreams.

We help in our own way to make a better world. We like to use nature in our lives and in the lives of those close to us. This has proved to be very beneficial to us!

Is it not our true nature to live in balance with the many life forms and energies that surround us? We should maintain balance in our lives in order to be happy and attract what we desire. Nature can reveal so many secrets and help us reach that balance.

Life has not always been easy for my family and I. When Sylvain and I met, we had nothing, except for Sylvain's car, a Dodge Charger, and my sewing machine. But what we did have, was an intense love for one another. Without money, but full of hopes and dreams, we got married at 21. I had no job and Sylvain worked as a heavy equipment operator.

We decided we wanted a big family (Oh, yeah, 8 children, it was pretty ambitious for that time). I loved children so much. I did not know how we would get there, but I knew very well what I ardently desired. And so, our desire was launched into the Universe...

I started working in IT (information technology) for the government. After two years, we moved into our first house and a year later, Vanessa increased our family, making us happy parents.

During the years that followed, I had three miscarriages. It was a difficult period for us, since both of us wanted a big family. After numerous medical tests, I was officially declared... "infertile". In my constant quest for a solution, I looked beyond traditional medicine.

I discovered kinesia therapy, a very new science at the time. At my first visit, my practitioner, who was also a chiropractor, told me that a problem with my spine was blocking irrigation of my reproductive organs. After a few treatments, everything was back to normal and I was also pregnant again. I continued these treatments throughout my pregnancy and even afterwards.

At the 40th week of my pregnancy, my baby decided he was not ready to leave his little nest. In agreement with my doctor, we decided to let the baby come according to his own rhythm. At 42 weeks, an ultrasound revealed that my baby was not looking good. She had changed her position and so I had to have a cesarean. The operation was performed that very same day by a team of specialists. My daughter Kaïla was put in my arms for a few wonderful moments. I was overwhelmed with joy!

But something was wrong... She was dark burgundy and breathed very heavily without making any sound... Her neck was bigger than her head. It was so big. Her body barely moved. I did not have the joy of holding her against me for very long, since she was taken away immediately and placed under observation.

I could not see her afterwards, since she was transferred to a specialized children's hospital. I was overwhelmed when they informed us of her transfer. I could not even hold my child in my arms to comfort her and I could not get around by walking, due to complications from my cesarean.

My husband and I were told that Kaïla was to be kept in an incubator because of breathing problems that resulted from obstruction of the airway. This was caused by her prenatal position. The news about her health unfortunately did not stop there...

She was mute and her skull was too large. The conclusion was that she had "hydrocephalia", commonly known as: Water on the brain. We were told she would probably never walk and that her life expectancy was approximately of 10 years. To top it all off, we were informed that she had the body of a girl, but she was asexual. She would never be able to reproduce because she was missing some of her sex chromosomes in the blood.

We were completely shattered. Especially, since I could not hold my baby. She was so far away... I needed her so much and she also needed me.

Upon my discharge, I was finally able to visit my little girl. For scientific research, the doctors asked to perform tests on Kaïla, advising us that it was not painful. For one of my visits, I arrived early and saw my little Kaïla with tubes in her throat, screaming in pain throughout her poor little body. Naturally, she made no sound, but her blue body was clenched, her small face contorted with pain, her eyes flooded with tears and her breathing was irregular and extreme, clearly demonstrating that she was in panic. It was a shock to see her suffer so. My body felt all of her pain. I was so frustrated that this could be done to my child.

The doctor tried to explain to me that it was not painful and that it contributed to the advancement of science. No words could convince the mother that I was and who felt what her daughter felt. Politely, I asked that all these tests be stopped. Following my refusal of treatment, the next day we got the hospital release for Kaïla.

What joy to take my baby home after more than a month of medical care. That day, I promised to myself to do whatever was best for my daughter, but in my way, following my own intuition.

Also, as a result, that day, without being conscious of it, I activated the powers of the Law of Attraction.

We had wanted this child so much and for so long. Now that Kaïla was finally home, we could share with her all our tenderness. I was convinced that in this environment filled with love, she could grow at her own pace surrounded by peace and harmony.

I had a few months of maternity leave before going back to work full time. With Vanessa, her big sister, we played "*Act as if...*". As if Kaïla could sing, dance, walk and play with us. For example, when we danced, I took Kaila in my arms and said "*That's it, Kaïla, that's perfect! Dance with us. One more step, like that. Go ahead, move your arms ...*". And we believed in it, Vanessa and I. We played it so often. Vanessa enjoyed inventing new scenarios and I joined in her games with my childlike heart. In her big eyes, Kaïla seemed to understand what I was doing. They were so deep, those eyes!

Every day, I took long walks outside with the girls. I loved fresh air, contemplating nature and enjoying the diversity, abundance and life. I gave thanks for all these blessings. I focused my attention on the opportunity to enjoy all of this and I shared my joy with my family.

Sometimes, I had moments of discouragement, and I cried and prayed. My older daughter Vanessa would come to me to console me tenderly, as a 5-year old child knows so well how to do. Children understand so many things. I'm always amazed. They are real life teachers, when we know how to recognize their teachings.

Sylvain was also always there to see how his daughters were progressing. After dinner, he would lay on the carpet, on the floor, and play "amusement park rides" with the girls. This is what Vanessa liked to call her favorite game. The girls loved playing with their dad. They climbed on him and he flew them around with his arms. We laughed a lot during these times.

After a few months, I asked Sylvain to take me to the Basilica of Ste-Anne-de-Beaupre in Quebec. I felt inspired to go there. The very next day, our entire little family left for Ste-Anne-de-Beaupre.

On entering the Basilica, wonderfully decorated with artistic works, I always feel a strong and benevolent energy. So many healings have taken place here. Sylvain went with Vanessa to go pray in a church pew.

I, with my little Kaïla silent in my arms, went straight to the magnificent statue of Ste-Anne in the front of the church. I do not know why, but I was attracted to this location. I had now become accustomed to following my inspiration. I came here without expectations, but for comfort.

I closed my eyes and spontaneously prayed with all my being.

"Holy Ste-Anne, I entrust to you my little girl whom I love so much. Accept her as your child. I, as an earthly mother can do no more for her than to love her with all my strength and to protect her. I see a future so promising for her, but I can't offer it to her. Be her mother, good Ste- Anne, you who have access to a realm which I can only dream of. You are the one my child needs. I therefore offer my child to you. May you make her a messenger of peace! I put my trust in your hands and I let go! Thank you for hearing my prayer". Eyes closed and full of tears, I raised my child in the air to offer her to Ste-Anne.

I cannot explain what happened to me after that. It was so unreal!

I felt myself lifted into a cloud of bright and peaceful light! Everything was perfect, I felt so good... I felt safe. I do not know how long this warm and soothing body wrap lasted. After regaining my senses, I was in the same place in the Basilica, in front of the statue of Ste-Anne with my child tight against my heart... And I started crying, swept with joy and emotion...

Without understanding what was happening, I had let go by entrusting my child to Ste-Anne.

When I met Sylvain and Vanessa, I excitedly asked them if they had seen the comforting light that had surrounded and lifted me. They hadn't been looking in my direction. They had not seen anything and found this story a bit strange.

I was feeling so good and crying with joy! They saw and felt the emotion that I was emitting. They wanted more information. Vanessa, with the imagination of a five-year old girl, picked up my story.

As we left the church, a new reality, full of magic, awaited us. Kaïla, unknowingly, actually gave us the greatest gift we can hope for. She began to cry and we heard the first cries of her short life. The tearful cries of an infant, that were so sweet to my ear. Her vocal cords were back to life! We were overwhelmed with gratitude! I burst into tears ... filled with happiness!

It was a miracle! After that day, miracle after miracle occurred...

A few days later I received a call from my doctor telling me that the latest medical analyses did not reveal anymore hydrocephalus syndrome and strangely, he read in the report that she had her sex chromosomes. She was truly a little girl who could reproduce, like all normal girls. I was amazed! In a just few days, Kaïla's medical situation had entirely reversed.

She was completely cured!!! She was our little miracle baby!

Kaïla's voice developed very quickly. She completely caught up with all the time lost. When she was six months, I finally decided to schedule an appointment with her doctor. I had canceled all my previous appointments.

I was in the waiting room when the doctor called Kaïla's name. As I got up, Kaïla began to cry louder than I had ever heard before. I tried to comfort her, but nothing worked. She seemed to be giving a demonstration of how well her vocal cords had recovered.

As I was gathering my belongings, the doctor realized that Kaïla was the patient he had called. He said that the child he had called was a baby who was mute. Politely, carrying Kaïla in my arms and going towards him, I put my handbag by his feet outside his office, near the waiting room. Kaïla's crying had now lowered in intensity. He asked me into his office. Gently, I shook his hand, mentioning that we had come simply to thank him for all that his team had done for my daughter. I asked him to close Kaïla's file, because it was our last visit. He said that he had never seen such a cure and that he was honored to have met us. Meanwhile, while I thanked all the staff, the other patients who were waiting in the waiting room began to applaud. It was so moving! This was our last visit to the doctors for problems connected to Kaïla's birth.

Subsequently, our family grew by 3 more girls. I have wonderful memories of these pregnancies, the births and everything that has followed. I also entrusted each of my daughters to our good Ste-Anne, as I did for Kaïla. Once in a while, I remind Kaïla that she can pray to Ste-Anne... She is her second mother.

Kaila, like each of her sisters that God has given us, has grown in wisdom and in beauty and filled with talent. Sylvain and I wanted eight children. I had eight pregnancies, including three miscarriages, but we have five beautiful daughters and our happiness is complete.

Sometimes Sylvain feels that he is in the minority... but that's another story!

SUCCESS IS SOMETHING THAT ONE LEARNS.

In this story, I have revealed an episode of my life in order to explain to you some specific steps that I have intuitively followed. In fact, during this period, I was somewhat isolated in my world, so I reconnected with nature and in doing so, I blossomed. I ultimately found my natural balance.

Subsequently, during the years that followed, on many occasions I applied these steps with success and have had very impressive results. Now I enjoy using them to attract all kinds of things or situations into my life. It's really exciting! I also developed several different tools that I wish to share with you.

If I can do it, you can too.

You just need to follow the steps and assimilate some very simple principles and then put them into practice.

Recommended Actions

Get closer to nature by a walk in fresh air and
become energized by the treasures of nature.
Soak it up regularly and
you will be ready for your new life.

Chapter 3

I take control of my life

*T*he Universe supports those who take control of their lives!

If you make the effort to organize and improve your life, you will be amazed to see that the Universe is doing everything to support you.

To start with, smile and laugh more. This will expand a happiness feeling that allows you to feel good. This is the starting point of your transformation. Lighten up your face with a radiant smile and you will become a stimulating energy, just like the sun, for yourself and for others that surround you.

I wrote this book in order to help you along your journey. It can be used as a learning tool or simply as an inspirational guide.

At the end of each chapter, there will be recommended actions. These are simple exercises that will allow you to put into practice the concepts in this book.

KNOWLEDGE ALONE
WILL NOT CHANGE
OR IMPROVE YOUR LIFE.
YOU MUST PUT THIS KNOWLEDGE
INTO PRACTICE,
TAKE ACTION!

It is for this specific purpose that this advice is offered to you. I mention it often: it is through actions that the desired changes will occur.

In addition, it would be wise to use a file folder or binder in which you could insert and keep the written exercises. It is always nice to have all your exercises together in one document. This way, you can measure your progress, development and success after a certain period of time.

You can also use this book without doing the exercises. This still introduces you to the concepts. Some people prefer to read the whole book first and then return later to the chapters that held the most attraction for them. You know better than anyone which way suits you to learn best. Follow your instincts. The more you put these concepts into practice, the better the results you will get.

You can expect improvements if you apply these concepts. *The Universe must deliver* what you focus your attention on. I will guide you so that you can attract the positive into your life. However, the results depend totally on you.

Also, you will notice that I often use certain concepts repeatedly. I assimilate information a lot better when my mind receives it repeatedly. Our subconscious works in the same way and it is for this reason that I have inserted some key elements into the text.

Our team is constantly developing new tools to help people evolve more quickly. Many of these tools are free. You can visit our Website to use this material. We also offer workshops and seminars in natural settings where you can enjoy nature and/or horses. Several training tools have also been developed so that you can use them at your convenience, no matter where you are. www.abundancethrunature.com

☯ Recommended Actions

Reserve a folder or an exercise workbook for
your recommended action exercises.
And above all, become inspired and smile.
Do not forget to take action...

27

Chapter 4

Dreaming of a better life

*E*veryone aspires to a better life!

It is normal and natural to always want more out of life. In nature, everything also grows and increases.

Everything is in constant movement in the world. Even the smallest of particles is constantly in motion. Everything is energy, even our thoughts. Every thought has a vibrational frequency (of energy), which draws and attracts its equivalent. In addition, the higher the vibratory frequency is, the closer it is to love. And therefore, this vibration becomes more powerful. This reality is now supported by the science of Quantum Physics.

Now, let's clarify certain concepts in order to manifest the changes that we want to see happening in our lives.

Your brain is made up of two very distinct elements that manage your thoughts and beliefs. It is important to note that your beliefs always have priority over your thoughts.

A) *The conscious mind*: It is responsible for daily living. You control your thoughts through your will. You can use the conscious mind through your willingness to change the beliefs stored in your subconscious.

B) *The subconscious mind:* is your storehouse of information. It also contains your beliefs and doubts. Its main task is to protect you. To do this, it uses the information you have submitted to it at any given moment, in specific circumstances. This information serves as a reference for the subconscious mind, and has usually been accepted without ever being questioned. Your subconscious works without your will being able to control it.

90% of your mental life is unconscious.

Your subconscious mind always refers to information that has been stored in your mind. However, sometimes this information is no longer valid and you should replace it so you can evolve and improve your current life.

**YOUR SUBCONSCIOUS
DOES NOT KNOW
THE DIFFERENCE BETWEEN
WHAT IS REALITY OR
WHAT YOU TELL IT
TO BELIEVE.**

So you can condition your mind to believe what you want it to believe, so that the new conditioning becomes a new reality for it. Your subconscious mind will use this new reference as it requires it. By reprogramming the subconscious mind with new references, you can propel your life and your reality.

Your subconscious mind can solve any problem or question, if you manage it properly.

Let's take an example to explain this. If you want to build your dream home, your basic plans would be developed very thoroughly and the materials would be very carefully selected. You would examine every detail and correct them if necessary until they reflected your dreams perfectly.

Why are we not as selective about our mental house? It is so much more important than the house we live in. Everything that appears in our life depends on the materials used in the construction of this mental house.

You must select your thoughts with great care since they become the references that the unconscious mind uses and ultimately these thoughts create your life. Store optimistic, creative and positive thoughts, and maintain these thoughts. Do the housekeeping in your mental house by eliminating thoughts that are not stimulating. You must keep your mental house always clean.

Seek out silence. In silence you will find peace and rest. A rested mind can generate creative thoughts.

These thoughts, however, require an effort of concentration.

The more you practice thinking about how to attract abundance, the easier this will become. You will then be conditioned to do it automatically.

THE REAL BATTLE OF LIFE
IS SIMPLY A
BATTLE OF
YOUR IDEAS

Now that you understand the importance of choosing the thoughts that you allow to stay in your mind, here are some very beneficial tips.

- Feel love and share love. You will feel so good.

- Watch TV programs that are stimulating and rewarding. Avoid violent and demoralizing programming.

- Spend most of your time living your own life rather than watching others live their lives.

- Avoid the news, especially just before going to bed. This kind of negative information negatively programs your subconscious mind while you sleep.

- Instead, look for positive and relaxing information and activities before going to sleep.

- Spend time doing what you love and what generates beautiful thoughts, such as spending time with your friends and positive people.

- Avoid the media that conveys messages of lack, sickness, misfortune and catastrophes. You do not want to expose your thoughts and emotions to this negative information.

- Stop comparing yourself to others. Appreciate who you are.

- Create, stay busy. The act of creation generates energizing thoughts.

- Keep moving, always continuing to evolve. Avoid stagnation.

- Avoid negative conversations.

- Learn to say "No".

- Avoid negative people who attract problems. Since energy is contagious, you do not want to catch their misfortunes.

- Enjoy nature with all the love that it is bathed in and tap into this regenerative energy.

By adopting these new habits, you will feel so much better. Most of all do not think that you are isolating yourself from reality. If you need to know what is happening in the news, there is always someone who can report the main headlines in a few words. You will have the information, but not to the extent and without the emotions conveyed by the media.

When your thoughts are constructive, positive and powerful, this will manifest itself in your reality, your health, your environment and your financial situation.

☯ Recommended Actions

Remain vigilant about your conscious thoughts
that you allow to live in your mental house.
Maintain your guard constantly
and this will be reflected in your reality.

Chapter 5

Awaken your passion

*E*verything you do with passion will fulfill you.

If you keep doing what you do, but you do not feel any happiness in doing it, you cannot live happily and to your full potential.

Your life is what it is, according to the choices that you have made. You can make new choices. However, to succeed in life, you have to make choices that make you feel good.

You are unique and you have talents you can share to benefit the others around you and even possibly the world. Find your passion. Passion is essential to achieve happiness, success and abundance.

But how do you know whether you will be passionate about something? It's simple. What you will be passionate about is whatever you feel good about when you think about doing it. It doesn't matter what it is. You can talk about it constantly, you put energy into it and you always want to learn more about it.

YOUR PASSION GIVES YOU ENERGY

Once you find a way to spend more time doing what you really love, you will feel fulfilled. It will bring you even more joy when you can earn money doing what you love. There is always a way to earn money when you follow your passion.

If you want to create the life of your dreams, you must spend a great deal of your time doing what you're passionate about and, ideally, generating the income that you aspire to have.

To sum it up, you must love what you do. You must feel love for everything around you: your environment, your customers, your talents, your creations, the equipment you use and everything else. The more you fill yourself of love for whatever you do and everything around you, the more you will attract even more of all these blessings.

Love is so powerful that it always attracts more of what you love. So, feel the love and nurture these powerful feelings for everything that you love, everything that you are passionate about.

Enjoy feeling the love with all your senses. Hear it, see it, taste it, smell it, speak it and sense it throughout your body.

Love everything as you love what you are passionate about and your life will be transformed in the most marvelous way.

At one time in my life, I noticed that my girls liked to go with me to the stable, but some of them had some fear of the horses. To make their experience more enjoyable, I began to introduce horse riding to them with very sweet, small ponies. I hired talented people qualified to share this knowledge.

Soon, I developed love for these small mounts, for the pony games, for the moments of joy and the complicity between the children and the ponies. I had so much love for everything and this allowed my children and all the other children and customers to learn in a serene and healthy way.

ANYTHING THAT IS EMPOWERED BY LOVE WILL GROW AND FLOURISH.

And so my love and passion grew. Along with my team, I have developed training materials and programs allowing the customers to learn how to ride by playing games on ponies and horses.

All this love acted like a magnet, attracting even more good things to us.

In short, I experienced pleasure, love and passion for this world. I rejoiced seeing the riders grow up in an evolving environment that could adapt to each stage of their development. My daughters experienced that pleasure and have developed a true love for horses.

This passion is such a part of them. It motivates them and gives them wonderful energy. However, this passion is not as strong for each of my daughters and this is fine since they all can make their own choices.

My passion for the equestrian world is always present. This passion grows and changes as I do. The services we offer in our riding school have also adapted to our development. This is a normal process. We grow with our passions, carrying it through our evolution.

We must never extinguish the flame of energy called: passion. So many people let their passion die off. I, on the other hand, encourage all passionate people to do what they love. This passion can transform itself and it is predictable. This is simply called evolution.

Too many people study and choose a career to please someone else. We cannot wish for someone to live our dreams. We all have to live our lives and we all aspire to live fully in joy and love.

As a parent, it is so beneficial to support our young people in the pursuit of their dreams and passions. We cannot ask our children to live the life that we have wished for ourselves. We should let everyone live their dreams, motivated by love in everything they do.

Happy people have the light of passion and love in their eyes. We cannot and must not extinguish the flame of love.

Recommended Actions

Discover your passion or passions.
Find the way to do what excites you
as often as possible allowing you to benefit
from this incredible energy.

Chapter 6

Positive thinking

*Y*our thoughts create your life, so you must think positively.

Constantly focus on your ideal life or situation as if it were already real. As you create your life through your thoughts, you have to think positively in order to attract all the good things that you aspire to.

Everything is within your power. This power acts in the present moment. You have been made to live a life of change, growth and well-being. You are the creator of your life.

If your life is not what you wish, you must understand that *this is what you have attracted.* Sometimes you do it unconsciously, with the beliefs that are ingrained in your subconscious mind. You are not even aware of these limiting beliefs that are found at the subconscious level. Conscious or not, your limiting beliefs can always be replaced by constructive beliefs that would support your objectives of personal growth. Your goal is to live and evolve, through the use of more creative beliefs. Your future will then be a reflection of your new positive thoughts.

Everything that exists in the air, on the land, in the water and in our bodies is vibration in motion. All of it is managed by the Law of Attraction. There is nothing that is not in movement. Our thoughts and emotions are also vibrations in constant motion and are managed by the Law of Attraction, like all moving particles.

The Law of Attraction responds to these vibrations and organizes them, bringing together the vibrations that are similar to each other, while keeping away the vibrations that are different. The lack of prosperity, happiness or whatever you are missing, simply means that you are emitting a different vibration than the vibration of prosperity or happiness. You cannot prosper while feeling poor, by emitting vibrations of poverty. Unless you produce a vibration of abundance, abundance will not come to you.

Inner abundance is the secret to attracting outer abundance.

I know it seems impossible to think *prosperity* when there is not enough money to pay for food and your bills are piling up. But it is possible, when you pay attention to what is in abundance all around you, in nature or some other place you choose. Continue reading and it will give you more ideas.

**YOU CAN CHANGE
YOUR CURRENT CONDITIONS
BY CHANGING YOUR
VIBRATIONS AND
YOUR THOUGHTS**

You just have to focus your attention on something that makes you feel good.

We, as humans, have extraordinary powers. By the power of our thoughts alone, we can create our dream life. Isn't this wonderful? So, let us begin our journey towards achieving our dream life.

Even if your dreams are evolving, which is quite normal and to be expected, the Universe will guide you in the right direction. You will only have to change your course to adapt to your path.

Let's begin with an overview of some concepts.

It is through our thoughts and not our actions, that we first create. Through thought, we activate the Law of Attraction. Our thoughts generate vibrations. Our thoughts, supported by strong feelings (emotions) amplify the vibrations. Emotions, whether positive or negative, are the most powerful vibrations.

To change your life story, you need to start telling a new version of it. You must *tell the story as you want it to be!* Not just here and now, but every day... This is your new way of living: to strive for abundance and to live your life.

START TO TELL A NEW VERSION OF YOUR STORY, AS YOU WANT IT TO BE.

Do not dwell on the past and your painful experiences. It serves no purpose and you will vibrate with the same harmful experiences that you are going to attract. You act like a victim. Victims never attract anything good. If this is your situation, perhaps is it time to change...

Refocus your attention on what you want in your life, that which makes you feel good. Feel the love for all the situations, things and people around you. Love makes you feel good. This is the only way to attract good things to you quickly. This is the basis of your attraction power.

Starting now, try not to put others responsible for your success or the lack of it, because when you do, you are acting like a victim. You will then be powerless to make any changes and you will stagnate. You will always remain in the same negative energy.

You have the ability to focus on what you want or what you do not want to have in your life. One of these choices propels you to attract good things, while the other, unfortunately, attracts misery and lack.

THE WAY YOU FEEL INDICATES THE CHOICES YOU ARE FOCUSING ON.

You can always change your choice so that you align yourself towards emotions that attract pleasant and constructive experiences in your life. I'm not saying that this is easy. It is certainly more difficult the first time, but if you persist, it will become a habit. I can assure you that you will quickly see results.

Throughout your journey, I will teach you how to change your perception of things, so as to attract abundance in your life and create the life you dream of.

Did you notice how dogs are always happy to welcome their master when he comes home? They await him patiently. If they have young masters who go to school and come back at a certain time, they are always at their post to offer them a warm welcome. When they see one of their masters, they wave their tail, stick to their side and wait for a kind word and a pat on the head.

Dogs see the positive in you. They are always happy to see you. You can also enjoy this positive side of yourself. You just have to concentrate on the positive things as your qualities.

Successful people do not think in the same way as people who stagnate.

To succeed, we must have a good self-esteem. Believe that we can do it. From this moment on, that's what you should believe.

So, focus your attention on directing your life and speaking positively about your life and your future. Your words organize your thoughts, hence the importance of choosing your words well.

☯ Recommended Actions

Starting today, talk about your life
as if it is as you wish it to be.
Avoid talking about all negative subjects.
Realize that you must have
a good self-esteem.
You can do it...

Chapter 7

My new wake-up

Each new day offers new possibilities.

Your choices are infinite. You can decide what you want to do with your life. But each day that begins offers you the possibility to build a new vibratory base which will set the general tone of your thoughts for the rest of the day.

When you awake, you are in an Alpha state of great relaxation, and you emit very strong vibrations. This is a period where the right and left brain work in harmony and therefore the whole brain is in a listening mode. You can use this period to improve your memory, increase your creativity and your knowledge and send new messages to your mind. When you're in an Alpha state, you have much easier access to your intuitive, creative and inspirational abilities.

It's smart to take advantage of this period as you begin your day.

This Alpha state is not only accessible in the morning and at bedtime. You can access it at your convenience when you put yourself in a state of deep relaxation.

For example, you can sit in a waiting room or relax on a bench in a park and simply let your body and your mind relax so you feel nice and calm. This feeling brings you closer to the Alpha state.

The majority of people who want to excel in different fields use these precious periods of the Alpha state to program their brains and their bodies.

I like to start my day when I am in an Alpha state, with my prayers and thanks to the Universe for all that is positive in my life. I call this my **gratitude time**. I cite things for which I am grateful, such as my comfortable bed, my health and the health of all my relatives, my family, my inspiration, my energy, my freedom, our healthy and delicious food, the sun that warms my skin, my clothes, the wonderful people around me, financial abundance, singing birds and so on...

Since we are again in an Alpha state just before going into a deep sleep at night, I have a period of appreciation at that time as well. However, in the evening I add one ritual before going to sleep. I like to note the things that I thank the Universe for. I always keep **my gratitude journal** right next to my bed. I sometimes write my thanks in the dark, when I prefer not to turn the light on. I cannot see what I am writing and in the morning, I sometimes find it difficult to reread. It does not matter...

The Universe knows what I have written. It is the intention and the energy that matters. As I mentioned often, I believe in the power of writing.

IT IS THE INTENTION
AND THE ENERGY
THAT MATTERS.

Since we always attract what we focus our attention on, it is logical to say that you are attracting, more and more, all those things for which you are sending out your gratitude. If I am thankful for my abundance of healthy and delicious food, I always attract plenty of healthy and delicious things to eat. It is like this, for everything you include in your gratitude. In addition to allowing you to attract your gratitude items in abundance, this habit will put you in the vibrational state that allows you to act as a magnet for what you want in your life.

The Universe is like a benevolent parent. If a parent offers special attention, like a movie night to her child and the child is truly grateful, won't the parent want to repeat such a gesture? Of course! In contrast, if the child does not like this evening and criticizes it in every way, do you think the parent will want to repeat the experience? Certainly not, since it was not appreciated. It is the same for the Universe. When you appreciate something it is so happy to give you more.

So make it a habit to give thanks for all the positive things you have in your life. We all have them. So there is no need to look very far. The sun shines for all. You only have to be aware and thankful for it.

You will notice that this habit develops with practice. As soon as precious moments happen in your life, immediately realize that you can be thankful for that. You can even note it in the evening in your **gratitude journal**. As you continue to be attentive to everything that may spark your gratitude, you will find that more and more things happen in your life for which you may be grateful.

For us, it's a habit to thank the Universe when something good happens in our lives. It is even more powerful when we express this gratitude out loud and with a lot of emotion. I am somewhat expressive and sometimes I thank the Universe with such intensity that I make my family laugh. This has now become like a game for us and everyone does it spontaneously. The energy created is really contagious. It allows us to feel good and to attract good things in our lives. Who doesn't want to have fun? Try it and you will see. A smile will light up your face.

Be thankful for the good and beautiful things or situations that brighten up your life and demonstrate this to the Universe in your own way.

Also be sure to savor every victory in your life. Small or great, they are all important. Each victory strengthens you and allows you to create bigger and more victories.

When I have a few moments, I love to enjoy nature, the behavior of people and animals, the movement of clouds, the beauty and perfection of vegetation and flowers, the power of the sun and the wind, the beauty of light waves of water with its reflections like diamonds on the surface. There are so many reasons to be thankful for and inspired by. It's magic when we enter this state of thankfulness for all blessings.

Find your own reasons to be thankful for and become like a young child who looks forward each day to the wonders he will discover in his universe.

This is really the state that we need to be in, as a child, amazed and contented by life.

Here is the first step of the process that I am proposing and that will let you to realize all your dreams. With this powerful Creation Process, I have attracted miracles.

"Touch of nature" Creation Process

STEP 1:
Be grateful for all
that is beautiful and good.

It is very important to understand now that: Gratitude must become a constant habit on your journey towards happiness and a life of abundance. You cannot achieve a life of abundance and plenty, if you do not express your gratitude on a daily basis.

GRATITUDE
IS REALLY POWERFUL.
IT MAKES YOU FEEL GOOD AND
ATTRACTS EVEN MORE
WONDERFUL THINGS!

To help you through dull times, take out your gratitude journal and enjoy a few passages. You will immediately begin to feel better.

Recommended Actions
Practice gratitude on a daily basis.
Become like an contented child.
Use your gratitude journal
to consult and become stimulated.

Chapter 8

Live in the present moment

*I*t's in the present moment that we can change our lives.

We are all creators. Yes, we have the power to create that which we desire. By paying attention to how we feel now, we can redirect our thoughts to generate feelings that will bring well-being to us.

When a situation is uncomfortable, stop and close your eyes if you have to. Touch something and realize you're in the moment and you are the creator of your life. Here and now, you can direct your attention to what is good for you. Say: "I want to feel good". Repeat it again and again in silence or out loud if you want. Go somewhere else if necessary. Avoid all tense situations and negative people.

THE PRESENT MOMENT WILL
NEVER COME BACK.
IT IS PRECIOUS AND UNIQUE.

Savor the beauty of the present moment. Be inspired by nature. Contemplate a tree, a bird, the sky or whatever can stimulate you. Admire the perfection of creation. Appreciate it, savoring each detail.

We rarely take the time to appreciate our life, here and now. It's when we start to appreciate and are grateful for the beauty in our lives that we reach a level of marvelous well-being and become a powerful magnet that attracts even more of what we desire.

**_IT IS SAD TO REALIZE
THAT SOMETIMES, IT IS WHEN
WE ARE AFRAID OF LOSING
SOMETHING PRECIOUS
THAT WE REALLY
APPRECIATE IT._**

There is no need to wait for something unpleasant to happen, to really appreciate what is dear to you. If there is someone who is dear to you, you can tell them how much they mean to you. Take advantage of birthdays and occasions, if you're too shy to tell them otherwise. You can write some kind words in a card or on a piece of paper that you can slip into a certain place where this person may discover it during the day. It is so heartwarming to know that you really matter to someone.

You deserve the best there is! Try to appreciate what you find around you, pay attention to everything you love, the best things. There is always something positive, even in situations that you may perceive as negative today.

Enjoy the present moment and what surrounds you, enjoy life, appreciate the people close to you, immerse yourself in the abundance that is in every breath you breathe. Smile and you will feel good. When you feel good, you vibrate and attract the positive in your life.

A walk in the country, a visit to a park, a moment of rest on a terrace, playing a game with your family, enjoying your friends or spending time with your pets, are just a few of the examples of "in the moment" happiness. Be inventive and find your own.

I can spend extended amounts of time in nature, breathing fresh air, hearing the birds singing and watching the behavior and interrelationships between people and/or animals. I appreciate these moments of peace and love and I am able to draw inspiring energy from them.

Seek out silence. Your power comes from rest and quiet, since this is what allows you to think. Your achievements are a reflection of your past thoughts.

Recommended Actions

Concentrate on the present moment
Find beauty in this moment and
be thankful for being conscious of it,
because it will never come back.

Chapter 9

You must feel good

W hen we feel good, life is so wonderful.

Feeling great makes us become magnets that attract the positive in our lives. You attract health, abundance, love, wealth, success or whatever you want. There you are, a wonderful excuse to feel good!

To feel good, you should search for reasons to feel good. We all have reasons to feel good. It could be because you are working on a project that excites you, because you're healthy, because you are wearing a new outfit that you like, because you've noticed new flowers in the garden... There are a multitude of reason to feel good at every moment. When you find the first reason to feel good, this nice thought will attract a second one, which will attract another and so on. You'll be in a positive and powerful vibrational state.

The simple act of reading this book right now may be a reason to feel good, because you finally understand the power you have over your life. Other energizing thoughts about your wonderful powers will follow this thought and you will be fully energized. When you feel great you will become a magnet that attracts the positive into your life.

Our body was created in a way that we can experience a multitude of emotions from each of our senses. Everything is in place to enable us to reveal different levels of emotions. We just need to learn to detect and analyze them.

The following is a list of some emotions presented in the book: The Power from Rhonda Byrne. This list begins with the emotions that produce the most positive and creative energy, which create a greater sense of well-being. The lower you go on the list, the more these emotions produce more and more crippling energy, creating discomfort, illness and other things that you do not particularly want to bring into your life.

Love
  Gratitude
  Joy
   Passion
    Excitement
    Enthusiasm
    Hope
    Satisfaction

        Irritation
        Worry
        Criticism
        Anger
        Hate
        Envy
        Guilt
        Fear

LOVE IS THE MOST POWERFUL OF EMOTIONS. LOVE PRODUCES MIRACLES

Do not let outside elements control your emotions. Even if it is raining or if your day does not go as you had hoped, you can feel good. Too many people let events dictate their mood. You have the power to change this. Take a deep breath and smile. In this way, you are taking the first step in the right direction.

If you allow negative thoughts to inhabit your mind, these thoughts will attract thoughts with the same vibrations and you're caught in a whirlwind of negative emotions. When you allow these negative emotions to inhabit your mind for a long time, you will experience a deterioration of your physical self. In other words, you will attract sickness or negative events.

When your thoughts are constantly negative, it is upsetting to realize that they can be absorbed into your subconscious mind and become a limiting belief. This will attract nothing good...

Let's take an example of animal behavior to explain how we can adapt ourselves to fit our emotions.

When a fly lands on the horse's skin, the horse reacts by moving the muscle under his skin at that exact location. The horse's body consists of a multitude of nerve endings which can detect the exact spot where the

59

fly has landed. The horse uses its tail to shoo the flies from those parts of his body. On the other hand, since it cannot shoo away the flies that land on the front of his body, it will frequently rub itself against another horse. You see, when horses are in the pasture and there are flies, they group themselves so that each may drive away the flies from the body of another horse. The tail of one horse may well drive away the flies from the front of the body of another horse. This support allows each horse to feel good, thanks to help from the other horses. And all of this happens in a very natural way.

Through appropriate behavior, the animals have learned to improve their conditions. They instinctively always try to feel good.

We should also always try to feel good. As humans, we have an advantage over the horses. We have power over our thoughts. It is by choosing our thoughts that we can generate creative and positive emotions that allow us to feel good.

Whenever you feel bad, you're attracting something that you do not want. It is as simple as that!

So learn to analyze tightness in your stomach, tension in your body, headaches and everything else. Your body is constantly talking to you. You have to learn to be more attentive to what it is saying. At first, it may seem very subtle and difficult to understand, but over time, it will become second nature and you will know immediately that it is time to change your focus of attention back toward more positive and creative vibrations. In addition, your body also will feel better than ever.

60

YOUR EMOTIONS
ARE IN MANY WAYS
THE GUIDES TO YOUR LIFE.

You must learn to feel and perceive your emotions. Then, you will be able to naturally analyze if you feel good. If you do not, you can easily change the situation. You have the power to do this.

Like the horses that contribute to the welfare of one another, you must feel good in order to create your own happiness and contribute to a better world.

☯ Recommended Actions
Be attentive.
You must feel good to attract
what you want in life.
Become aware of how you feel and
make sure you feel good.

Chapter 10

A powerful language

Our words attract our future.

To guide you towards positive language that will bring you the best results, I'll share some tips with you.

When you fix your attention on what you want, using positive words that you say often, your vibration will change and over time you will experience a transformation in the way you feel and you will be able to attract what you want into your life.

Listen to your words when you speak. Your words are always preceded by thought. If you find yourself in the middle of a conversation saying something contrary to what you desire, stop yourself and say: "*I know what I do not want. What do I really want?*". Then clearly affirm what you want by saying "*I want…*". This method allows us to change our focus to realign towards something positive that we want, rather than putting attention on a negative subject. Some people call this technique "pivoting your attention".

Many people know what they do not want. They talk about it and think about it a lot. In short, they focus their attention on what they dislike and do not want in their lives. Because they know what they do not want, they can use it to define what they do want.

From now on, try and listen to your words when you find yourself thinking and talking about what you do not like and do not want in your life, then replace them immediately by what you want.

For example:

- I am fat.
  replaced by: *I want* to be thin

- I am sick.
  replaced by: *I want* to be radiantly
  healthy.

With your affirmation "*I want...*", you put yourself into a positive vibration. Afterwards, answer "*Why*" you desire this, by involving your feelings. Everything is based on the intensity of your feelings.

Positive example:

> *I want* a bike.
> *Why?* Because I always feel good when I go out and peacefully admire the scenery. I hear the birds sing and enjoy the leaves moving gently with the breeze. Everything seems more peaceful and joyful. I like feeling happy. In such an environment, I picture my future with more moments like this and I smile. Life is so beautiful... I imagine our rides with friends when we discover new things and we enjoy life,

appreciating the good outdoors times. We are so free and we love to feel free.

While vibrating with such positive thoughts in your body, the Universe can only give you good things. You become a magnet for prosperity.

When you state your "*Why*", you must find the positive aspects of what you want to attract. Use words and feelings that make you vibrate positively and that make you feel so good.

In my example, I could have used something negative.

<u>Negative example:</u>

> *I want* a bike.
> *Why?* Because this would allow me to vent my frustrations when I see this city in ruins, full of dirt with its noisy traffic. Even if there are a few trees here, nothing is beautiful."

With words like that, you could never attract a bicycle, or anything positive, because you emit negative vibrations of scarcity. And that is precisely what you will attract into your life: frustration, shortage, traffic, noise and even ruins and dirt.

This example illustrates the power of your words and your attention. It is a powerful method that I propose you should master. Learn to dictate to the Universe what you want and sense it through your body, generating good feelings that allow your entire being to feel good. Make it an habit to use this method. You must understand the power of your words, your attention and your feelings. Through them, you create your life. This is really how the Universe works.

Now, above all, do not worry about:

-"*How?*" or
- "*When will this happen?*"

By placing your attention on these details, you return to the problem and to negative vibrations.

**LET THE UNIVERSE
DO WHAT IT MUST DO
AND DO NOT WORRY
ABOUT THE DETAILS.
THE UNIVERSE IS
SO POWERFUL.**

There is nothing the Universe cannot create. It can synchronize all things and events in ways that you cannot even imagine. So we need to focus our energies on defining, imagining and feeling what we want.

Choose thoughts that generate well-being for you and talk about what you want, avoiding speaking about what you do not want. This allows you to emit the vibrational frequency of abundance.

It is also wise to speak with respect about the Universe, God, Buddha or any other entity that you consider supreme. For this guide, I use the word: The Universe.

It is important to understand that the Universe cannot deliver to you what you want, if you cannot show respect. You must align your energy and vibrations in a positive way, through your words and your actions. It's a way of life that will enhance your life in a very positive way.

For example, in order to have a body radiating with health and full of vitality, you must appreciate everything that is beautiful in yourself. Do not focus your attention on what you dislike. To clarify this, here are some words you have probably already heard:

- I hate my hair.

- My face is full of pimples.

- I have fat thighs.

What do you think people who make such statements can attract? Unfortunately, they attract to themselves, even more of what they do not like. If, on the other hand, they mentioned what they would like and focused their attention on what is beautiful concerning their body, they would gradually be transformed to reflect this new reality. So, instead, try making the following statements:

- I am learning new ways to style my hair. I love my hairdo.

- My skin is getting better each day.

67

- My thighs are getting more and more firm and thin.

Also, some people believe that friendship permits the use of a language that denigrates other. Teenagers frequently say *"You're an idiot"* or *"You can't do it"*. According to them, this is part of their friendship code. Unfortunately, this friendship code can have ramifications in the future. People also end up believing what they hear repeatedly.

**THE WORDS THAT YOU
THROW OUT TO OTHERS,
YOU ARE SENDING OUT
TO YOURSELF,
BECAUSE EVERYTHING YOU SEND OUT
COMES BACK TO YOU.**

Experiments were conducted with plants. By complimenting plants, giving them good care and lots of love, it was noticed that these plants produced many more flowers and of a better quality than plants that do not receive compliment but receive the same basic care.

We are living beings, just like plants, and we are receptive to kind and constructive words. The Universe is also receptive to the energy conveyed by words. So we all benefit from having stimulating and positive remarks to attract positive events to us.

Calmly reprogram your consciousness regarding your way of thinking and talking, which are directly related to what you attract into your life. I'll explain a little later in this manual, how to formulate a clear intention to the Universe, as well as affirmations you can use that support this intention.

☯ Recommended Actions

On a daily basis, practice pivoting
your attention to a
positive version using
"*What do I want*" and "*Why*".
Give it "feeling".

Chapter 11

The power of writing

*T*hrough writing, we can deliver our messages to the Universe.

It is fascinating to witness the power of writing. When the girls were younger, I loved telling them that angels came to read what we write in order to bring these messages to the Universe. In this way, we could attract what we wanted, simply by putting it in writing.

I sincerely believe in the power of writing.

Especially when writing by hand. I know that computers and other electronic tools can help the writing process, but for me, I have noticed that when I write by hand, I get much better results. I do not know why. Perhaps because the pen or pencil is an extension of myself.

Often, after writing what I want with a pencil, I transpose everything into my computer. I love to write everything by hand first. For this book, I wrote chapter after chapter in my notebook. I know this is not as productive, but it's so powerful.

I would like to offer you an exercise that I occasionally do. It is fascinating how well it works!

Imagine yourself in the future. You are living your ideal life. Now, you are going to describe your ideal day. From when you wake up until you go to bed. Be as detailed as possible, describing your emotions and what you are feeling. Use all of your senses. It is very important to put this in writing. So go get a pencil or a pen and let yourself go. You will be surprised by the results.

The first time I did this exercise, I worked for the government in a job for which I had no passion. Like so many others, I saw no way out of this situation. Even if I wanted to leave this job, it was impossible for me to do so at the time and I could not see any other way.

I took my pen and started writing my perfect day.

I wake up full of energy. I say my prayers and have my gratitude period. I then get ready for my day before the girls wake up. Then I go into each of my daughter's rooms to gently wake them up. We make breakfast and eat together. When they leave for school, I do my morning exercise (walking or something else). I have a relaxing bath and I do some household chores (washing, cleaning, cooking, sewing) before going out to enjoy nature. I then pick up the girls from school, to eat at home or in a park, or I organize lunch with good friends. During the afternoon, I attend to my personal growth, organize new projects, meet people and take time to enjoy nature. Then I welcome the girls home from school and if need be, I help them with their homework while I prepare the evening meal. Sylvain arrives home from work and inquires about our day. During dinner, each tells his adventures of the day and we share in the joy. Together, we finish the chores and everyone has a bath or shower. This is the period of cuddles and games. I then have a few moments to myself and I relax (read, sew, listen to inspirational materials, discuss about various projects ...). After putting the girls to bed, I take time alone in my room to recharge. I fill my gratitude journal, I prepare my to do list with the outcomes I desire for my next day and I read. I go to sleep saying my prayers and I dream of all I want to attract into my life.

Surprising as it may sound, eight months later I was on leave and living this amazing life.

A few months earlier, when I was still in my government job, I could not imagine that life could be so sweet. Indeed, at this time of my life, total exhaustion forced me to leave my job. As some say, I broke down...

My body and mind needed a break. I could not accept that such a thing could happen to me. I thought I had control of my life, but everything changed so fast. It was such a humiliation. I could not even function normally. I could not even do my daily shores like cooking, cleaning, taking care of my kids… To walk 20 meters was like climbing a mountain for me now and I was crying all the time. Fortunately, I received help and I quickly regained my quality of life.

I realized something fascinating. I had told the Universe that I wanted to leave this job that I did not like and that took up too much time and energy in my life. I was no longer living at that time. I had become an automaton. I would never have left that job by myself.

I was too afraid... I had fear of not having the financial resources to meet our needs, fear of regret for leaving a secure job with a pension, fear of not knowing what to do with my life afterwards, fear of being ridiculed by those I knew, fear of not being supported by my family and friends, and so on... In short, I had oh so many fears...

But the Universe took me away from this job as I had asked and gave me as a bonus, financial indemnities and a lot of time for myself and my family. I benefited from this period of calm in my life and I also realized I would never return to this kind of work that took too much out of my life and for which I had no passion.

WHEN ONE DOOR CLOSES, A BIGGER AND MORE BEAUTIFUL ONE OPENS.

This period allowed me to refocus on one of my passions, which is: horses. I therefore went from a job as manager of major IT (Information Technology) projects to... stable manager. Who would have believed this? Especially, since I knew almost nothing about horses at that time... This was the beginning of a great adventure that is still going.

I have never regretted this change of direction in my life. I have found my natural balance, that is to say, a balance in life that allows me to enjoy life while I blossom professionally, emotionally and at every level.

This experiment was initially a failure and a tragedy for me. But looking back to every wonderful experience this has brought into my life, I can say it was a blessing. The Universe led me to a much more energizing and rewarding path. It had a vision for me. It had a plan much bigger than I could possibly imagine. I learned to trust the Universe. It is benevolent, powerful and is always there to support me. I feel so loved!

WE CAN CHOOSE
TO USE OUR TIMES OF TRIAL
TO GROW
AND FLOURISH.

This simple exercise of writing down your dream day may surprise you. You have nothing to lose and everything to gain by trying it. This can easily be done while waiting for the bus or to occupy your time between activities. If you really want to change your life, use the power of writing and begin the change that you aspire to.

Just try it...

☯ Recommended Actions

Write often.
Write down your ideal day.
Feel it and enjoy it.
and await the surprises to come.

Chapter 12

What do you want?

*B*efore anything else, you must know what you want to attract to yourself.

To help you know what you really want, it might be beneficial to realize what you don't want anymore. It is usually easier for us to say what we do not want and what we dislike in our lives. We've been conditioned to think this way. So let's use this to define what we want.

To help you know what you really want, it would be recommended to define what you no longer want or do not want in your life.

Here are two new steps of the Creation Process I propose.

"Touch of nature" Creation Process

STEP 2:
State what you no longer want.

STEP 3:
Define what you do want.
(I want – Why?)

By knowing what we no longer want, we can clearly define what we want.

In my personal story, when my daughter Kaïla was sick, what I no longer wanted was for her to be sick and in pain. As for my own desires, I did not want to live like this. I wanted to live life fully, with healthy children. This was clear to me. Once I knew this, I could define what I wanted.

I want

> *I want* I want a healthy and happy daughter and I want to enjoy life with her.

Why?

> So I can see her enjoy life and live it to the fullest. So I can grow with her and support her in her projects. Also, so I can enjoy her smiles, her development, her achievements and share her life path with her. Discover with her through the rhythm of her life, all the treasures she has to offer the world. And most of all, to love her with all my heart. I deserve what's best in my life and she does too!

YOU ALWAYS DESERVE
THE BEST
FROM LIFE.

Quite simply, that's the way I thought. I did not dwell on the negative side of things. I did not believe that my daughter Kaïla could have all these *differences*. I did not even register the word "hydrocephalia". My brain immediately dismissed it. I could never remember that word when I was talking about Kaïla. The brain is very powerful. I did not want this to be a part of my reality and my brain helped me in this desire. In preparing to write this book, I even had to do some research to find the actual diagnosis of Kaïla's illness and the medical term "hydrocephalia"

At the time of this experience, I was determined to change my reality. I had just welcomed to our world this wonderful baby girl whom we had desired for so long. I let my imagination go. Vanessa, who was only five years old, helped us to invent exciting imaginary scenarios. I dove into these games and we had the most wonderful times.

Life was so beautiful! It is just this kind of thinking that has created such a beautiful life for us. Use this approach to clearly define what you want. Again, here are two steps of the process that I propose:

"Touch of nature" Creation Process

STEP 2:
State what you no longer want.

STEP 3:
Define what you do want.
(I want – Why?)

Only create ideal desires. Beautify and enrich your thoughts and the Universe will manifest your outer world to match the inner world that you create in your mind.

You cannot attract anything if your intentions are unclear. The Universe cannot guess what you want and because of this, it cannot deliver it to you. Take the time to formulate what you want. It is also strongly advised to put it in writing. The power of writing is undeniable.

**FOR THE UNIVERSE,
IT IS NO MORE
DIFFICULT TO CREATE
SOMETHING BIG
THAN IT IS TO CREATE
SOMETHING SMALL.
SO THINK BIG!**

Aim for the stars and you can reach the moon.

However, I must warn you. Be clear and firm when you decide what you want. Your subconscious mind or your ego may try to make you change your mind or make you doubt the validity of your choice. This is perfectly natural. Your ego is there to help you survive and as soon as you try to move in a direction that is somewhat unknown to it, it will interpret this as a danger. But you have power over that ego and you can convince yourself of the validity of your choice.

If you say, with energy and conviction "*I WANT*" (for example: "*I want* this house"), the Universe will begin to synchronize events, people and situations so that you can access what you want. You cannot even imagine what the Universe can do for you.

However, if the next moment you say: "*I could never allow myself to have this house*", or "it may be too early" or "*I think, I prefer to live in an apartment because there is less responsibility...*", then the Universe stops everything it has begun.

Sometime later, you come back in force and with conviction and you say: "*I want* this house". The Universe will, once again, begin to synchronize events, people and situations so that you can access what you want.

Again, doubts arise, and you mention and feel that you do not really want this house. The Universe, once more, stops everything.

The Universe is patient and always responds to your vibrations, but after a while it becomes confused when your energies are also all confused. You really need to know what you want.

Any uncertainty regarding your desires will create delays in their manifestation. Sometimes, your doubts may even cancel your request. Be clear about what you want and hold onto this vibration. This will facilitate and activate the realization of your desire.

Recommended Actions

Decide now, what you do want.
Be clear and put it in writing.
Then maintain a positive vibration
and a constant desire, with lots of love.
Above all, believe strongly that you will receive it.

Chapter 13

Your strong intention

*W*e all have an ultimate goal, our personal intention.

This ultimate goal is your "strong intention". It can also be your new-year's resolution that you want to treat more powerfully. Whatever you want can be your intention.

When you are motivated by a burning desire, you will be inspired to achieve your goal. This desire must come from deep within your being. You must be sure you can do everything that needs to be done in order to achieve this goal.

Some people intuitively know what they want. Others, on the other hand, are confused. They do not really know. The answer is within you. Ask yourself: *"What do I really want?"* The ideas will come naturally if you know how to listen. Sometimes it's very subtle.

This intention may change as you evolve.

Nothing is set in concrete, everything changes. And it is perfect this way!

Here is the fourth step in the process that I propose:

> ## "Touch of nature" Creation Process
>
> ### STEP 4:
> ### Develop your intention (your desire) and put it in writing.

To submit your strong intention, I recommend using the method presented in the book "Think and Grow Rich" by Napoleon Hill. I have read this popular book several times and I strongly recommend it.

Here are some rules you must apply to formulate your intention:

1. Formulate your intention in the present.

2. Before mentioning your intention, declare to the Universe: "**Every day in every way, I am getting better and better**".

3. Then start the intention with: "**I am so happy and grateful now that I am....**".

4. Set a date for which you aim to realize your desire. Be realistic and optimistic. If you are not comfortable about setting a date, simply don't. It is best not to set a deadline, if you think you will become

discouraged if your intention is not realized as the date approaches. Because in that case, you will transmit negative vibrations that will cancel your intention. The Universe often surprises us. It may deliver for you at the very last moment, but it is important to believe that it is possible, until the end.

5. Stipulate what you plan to offer in return for the realization of your intention. Everything is balanced. You have to give in order to receive.

THE UNIVERSE IS HERE TO HELP YOU AND DO WHAT IT HAS ALWAYS DONE: CREATE.

Let's look at some examples:

a) I am so happy and grateful now that I am glowing with health and have a healthy body that moves perfectly for the....*date*. In return, I promise to visit each month, children who are struggling to overcome cancer and encourage them in their journey.

b) I am so happy and grateful now that I am the owner of a successful company that generates increasing profits of hundreds of thousands of dollars, year after year, beginning today the... *date*. In return, I pledge to open a day care on site to improve the quality of life for the families of our employees.

c) I am so happy and grateful now that I am in a relationship with the ideal partner with whom I can increase my love and reach my dreams for the... *date*. In return, I pledge to continue my journey of personal growth which allows me to constantly improve myself and contribute to make a better world.

Now, write your intention. This intention will guide your choices and your actions, leading you towards your ultimate goal. This intention must produce a lot of passion and pleasure. You now have an ultimate goal and the Universe is there to assist you.

You can set intentions for every aspect of your life:

- Intellectual
- Physical
- Family
- Professional life
- Finances
- Spiritual dimension
- Social

Too many people do not know what they want in life. The Universe then cannot synchronize and organize events, people and situations which would propel them to the top. They let themselves be carried away by the river of life without being aware that they are masters of their craft and that they can direct it to their desired destinations.

YOUR INTENTION MUST GENERATE A BURNING DESIRE INSIDE OF YOU.

You have now understood this principle and you have taken control of your destiny by writing your intentions. The forces of the Universe are now willing to do what they have always done: Create.

Create what your mind has decided that should happen. Above all, do not try to tell the Universe "*How*" to do things. We have a very limited view of the infinite powers of the Universe. Concentrate on what you want and let the Universe do its work. I'm always surprised by the ways the Universe uses to make things happen in my life. It is usually much more and even better than what I had hoped for.

To help you activate your desire, you can write your intention on a small card. You can keep it with you to remind you of your intention. You can place this card in your pocket and when your hands come into contact with it, your subconscious mind will remind you of your intention. You could also keep it in your purse or wallet. The goal is to see it several times a day, so as to activate the mechanism of automatic thoughts.

You can also put your intention in writing next to your computer, make it your homepage on the computer, or leave an automatic call back on your electronic devices. You can find your personal method for leaving reminders of your intention. Each of these methods is as good as another. Go with what suits you best.

By defining your intentions, you are among the few who have a direction in life. Now let your intense desire inspire you to action.

☯ Recommended Actions

Write your intention
that generates a burning desire in you.
Store this writing in a place where you
you can use it as a reminder.

Chapter 14

Define your affirmations

P recision facilitates the realization of your desires.

When you order from a catalog, you know exactly what you want. In life, it is the same. The precision of your statements (that which you desire) is very important. Make sure you know the details of what you want and formulate your affirmations precisely.

An affirmation is a positive statement aimed at a specific target. In other words, you express your intention to do or be something specific. The positive statements regarding the intention or purpose that you want is used to reprogram your brain to achieve the desired results. The more you use them, repeat them and do this with conviction and emotion, the more you accelerate the process that allows your brain to accept it and then allow the Universe to deliver.

You have defined what you want (with: *I want* and *Why?*). Then, you have defined a clear intention, a direction for your life. You must now define the affirmations that support your intention.

AFFIRMATIONS HELP
TO REPROGRAM
YOUR SUBCONSCIOUS MIND
TO ACHIEVE
YOUR GOALS.

Here is the fifth step in the process that I propose:

"Touch of nature" Creation Process

STEP 5:
Formulate affirmations
that support your
intention (desire).

To enable you to establish clear and powerful affirmations, you must follow some rules:

1. Put your affirmations in writing.

2. The verb should be in the present tense.

3. Make the statements short and clear.

4. Write it personally, in the first person singular. Talk about yourself. Example: I am, I attract, I have...

90

5. The statement should reflect the situation as you want it to be.

6. Only state what you want. Do not mention what you do not want. Your subconscious eliminates the negative form. It makes everything into a positive form. Do not say: "I would like not to be afraid of dogs". Instead, make your affirmation in the following manner: "I'm comfortable with dogs and they like me."

7. You can make your affirmations the way you want, but you have to believe them. If you want to attract a certain sum of money in a given period, you must believe that this is possible. If not, your subconscious will not join in with the belief to achieve what you want. If you earn $ 5000/month and you want to attract $100,000/month, perhaps this increase is a bit too much for your subconscious mind. Be careful, it is important to clarify that for the Universe, nothing is impossible. However, it is also a matter of the beliefs you have. If you do not think this is possible, proceed gradually. Aim for an amount you think is possible, for example $6,000/month. When the goal is reached, you can move on to a next step of your staircase and set a new goal.

    This rule, believing that your statement is realistic to achieve, applies to all your affirmations and intentions that mention the quantities of a given thing. If your goal is too difficult for your subconscious mind to accept, proceed gradually, in small steps.

Here are some examples of affirmations:

- I am now perfectly healthy and I enjoy life.

- I make at least three new sales every day.

- I share my life with the perfect partner.

- My friends are sincere and good.

- I pass all my exams easily.

- I feel better and better each day.

- My clients are satisfied and always refer more customers to me.

- I live in peace and calm.

- Money comes to me in abundance, like the air I breathe.

- Every day I am getting closer to my ideal weight.

Now that you have made concise and precise affirmations about what you want, I will give you some little tips to increase their vibrations. We have already mentioned that our words, our thoughts and emotions are vibrations. Since everything is vibration and the Law of

Attraction is infallible, we must strengthen the vibration of our affirmations to enable them to be realized in our lives.

Here are a few tips. Adapt them in whatever way suits you. Be comfortable with the way you do it.

a. Make your statements out loud so you hear them. If you are alone, you can do it with intensity. Ideally, say them at least twice a day: in the morning when you wake up and in the evening before going to bed. You can also say them several times a day. The more occupied your brain is with your affirmations, the more quickly your subconscious will adopt them.

b. You can even sing your affirmations. I like to do this when I'm alone in my car. I sing with conviction. Motorists who pass me must think I am out of my mind. I have fun... and I can assure you that I generate a lot of vibrations.

c. Try looking in the mirror while you say your affirmations, this is even better.

d. When you formulate your intentions, put your hand on your throat or your heart to feel the vibrations. This way the energy circulates more strongly through your body. I like to put my hand on my heart while saying my affirmations.

e. Put some emotion into it, so you can multiply your vibration. Be inventive. Feel the joy of having already achieved your goal.

f. You can make your affirmations while you are exercising. I like to make my affirmations when I walk, dance or jump on my mini trampoline. I put on my headphones and listen to taped affirmations and I repeat them aloud while I am training. It's really energizing!

g. Use your imagination to see your affirmations already realized. Imagination is very powerful. The more you practice using your imagination, the easier it will become to use it. We offer tools that let you use your imagination to visualize your goal as already reached. This can be useful in getting used to using your imagination.

h. To remind you to think about your affirmations, you can write them down and post them in different places where you can see them during the day.

i. On your computer or electronic equipment, it is also possible to view or hear your affirmations. There are various tools on the market that offer different options. You can also leave the affirmations running as background noise or as a background video, while you go about your business.

j. I created a video with my affirmations and songs. I like to listen to it and watch it in the morning while I am getting ready. It makes me want to dance and that is such a great way to start the day!

TO ANCHOR YOUR AFFIRMATIONS IN YOUR SUBCONSCIOUS YOU MUST FEEL THEM.

There are also many tools on the market with written or pre-recorded affirmations designed for different aspects of your life: health, happiness, love, abundance, money, fitness, weight loss...

☯ Recommended Actions

Write your affirmations.
Repeat them with conviction and emotion.
Visit our website
www.abundancethrunature.com
for tools that allow you to vary the way
you anchor your affirmations
in your subconscious mind.

Chapter 15

Absolute certainty

*D*ecide now that your desires will be realized!

In Canada, where I live, we experience quite a change in the climate related to the seasons: winter, spring, summer and fall.

In winter everything is going at a slower pace. All of the elements of nature are asleep. The landscape is white, some animals hibernate, some have migrated to warmer climates and some others live in slow motion.

In spring, the snow melts, the first flowers appear, all of nature awakens and the sap flows out of the maple trees and we make it into maple syrup. The days are longer and we become energized. It is the beginning of a cycle. It's time to sow. It is also the season of love.

In summer, the sun warms nature and also our hearts. Everything is so beautiful and inspiring. This is the period of family vacations and projects. We have energy and we want to enjoy those long sunny days.

In the fall, everything slows down. It's back to school for children and the resumption of everyday life. It's the season for crops. The trees drop their leaves so they can come back stronger and more beautiful next spring.

We live to the rhythm of these seasons. Nature has confidence in cycles of creation. These cycles are powerful, constant, and always produce growth. We must understand that the Universe does the same for us.

WE MUST ADAPT AND FOLLOW THE RHYTHM OF THE SEASONS OF OUR LIVES.

If the Universe is able to synchronize all these developments to the smallest detail, we must believe it can do the same with our desires.

Here is the sixth step of the process that I propose:

"Touch of nature" Creation Process

STEP 6:
Believe with certainty
that it is possible.

Keep your focus on your desires, and continue to believe and you will obtain them. When concerns arise in your mind, realign your focus to more positive thoughts.

Sometimes, nothing goes right in your life. You make efforts, using the actions recommended in this book, but it seems ineffective. Results do not happen as you hoped they would.

Above all, do not give up!

Too many people give up and let events dictate their lives and their future. You deserve much better. You are the creator of your life!

As we have mentioned a few times, we attract experiences with our thoughts and emotions. If you have harbored thoughts of lack and problems for many years, it may take some time for the Universe to reorganize everything. However, depending on the strength of the creative energy with which you vibrate now, the Universe may also make your new reality materialize right away. You must believe in your dreams and maintain constructive thoughts.

**BY MAINTAINING VIBRATIONS
OF LOVE AND
POSITIVE THINKING,
YOU TRANSFORM YOURSELF
ON A CELLULAR LEVEL.**

When I was a child, I had a catapult (slingshot). It consisted of a small piece of wood in the shape of a Y to which was attached a rubber band that connected the two top ends together. The vertical part was the bottom handle. Holding the slingshot in one hand, with the other hand, you held a pebble against the elastic. By pulling the rubber band with the pebble towards you, you aimed at a target. When you let the elastic go with the pebble, it flew towards the target. The further the elastic was stretched, the further the pebble could be propelled.

When I'm in a period where I feel like I am going backwards and desires are slow to materialize, I imagine myself in a catapult (slingshot). I am the pebble. The further the situation appears to be from my goal, the more my elastic is stretched.

The Universe is waiting for the right time to propel me very far. And when I am projected towards my goal, the Universe always delivers more than I had hoped for.

For me, goals that are slow to materialize simply mean that the Universe is stretching my elastic preparing a flight into something magical. This is one of my beliefs. Since this belief is stored in my unconscious mind, my outside world delivers this reality to me.

Always continue to believe in your ideals, maintaining high frequency vibrations that generate positive and creative energy. Keep the faith. Remember my example of a slingshot with you as the pebble. You will soon be propelled toward your dreams...

☯ Recommended Actions

Believing is an important element of
the creation process. To help you through
moments of discouragement,
imagine yourself in the slingshot.
You will soon take off on your magical flight.

Chapter 16

Imagination allows you to visualize

*T*hrough imagination, you can create your life!

The Universe is very powerful. Our capacity to use our imagination through our minds often lessens with age. Perhaps it is because we use fewer and fewer of these capacities as we grow older.

Children have the facility to create an imaginary world that is theirs alone. They often also have imaginary friends and frequently invent their own adventures based on what they have seen, heard or experienced. As they grow older, children sadly abandon these talents that allowed them to use their imagination. This is usually caused by the pressures of society, the family, or any other entity, near or far, that influences the ideas of the young.

**VISUALIZATION SUPPORTED
BY POWERFUL EMOTIONS
TURNS YOU INTO A
PROSPERITY MAGNET.**

The reasons that have led you to neglect your capacity to use your imagination are not important, because you can train your mind to access it on demand. The more you practice and let your mind access your imaginary world (to create ideal situations, people and things), the more you will become a magnet for prosperity.

Here is the seventh step of the process that I propose:

"Touch of nature" Creation Process

STEP 7:
Visualize your life
with your intention
already realized.

I suggest the following exercise to help you develop these capabilities that will allow you to access your imagination.

This visualization tool is very powerful. It awakens all of your senses through your imagination. You can practice it as often as you like. It is adaptable to all situations.

It is highly recommended for when you're in bed and you cannot get to sleep. You will then sleep peacefully, emanating positive vibrations that attract good things into your life. This free recorded visualization is available on our website.

So let's begin this visualization:

Lying on your back, or sitting with your feet flat on the floor, place your hands comfortably with your palms facing the sky. Close your eyes and relax all of the muscles in your body, one after the other, starting with your toes, your ankles, calves, knees, and thighs. Continue upward gently, peacefully releasing all tension from your body, your back, your torso and your arms. Continue to your neck, your ears, the muscles in your mouth, your jaw, your cheeks, your eyes and eyebrows. You are now completely relaxed. You are breathing slowly and regularly. With each breath, you feel a wave of relaxation from your head that travels throughout your body, ending up at the tips of your feet.

Now, take a first breath by inhaling air from the abundant Universe, holding it, and then releasing it slowly as you also release all remaining tension and negative feelings. Inhale again, hold it, and release it slowly. Let's do it again, inhale the abundance, hold it, and release it slowly, freeing you from all negative feeling that remains present. You are now perfectly relaxed and peaceful.

Now visualize the following:

You find yourself in a room with a ceiling above you. Everything is dark and calm. With a light breath of air, the ceiling opens to create a passage. A weak light illuminates the opening in the ceiling. A staircase quietly lowers in front of you. On an impulse of curiosi-

105

ty, you gently get up from your position and you go towards the staircase. Calmly, you put your naked foot on the first step of the staircase. Everything seems so real. You hesitatingly climb up each of the steps.

When you can see through the opening of the ceiling, a fog hides your view, but everything seems peaceful up there. You continue climbing the stairs and you put your foot on the ground in front of the stairs. Under your feet, you can feel the sweetness of fresh new grass. What is hidden in this mysterious place? Slowly the mist clears to reveal a wonderful sight! You realize that you are accessing a Garden of Eden, a sort of paradise.

All around you, a garden is full of flowers carefully placed between the trails and protected by a few large majestic trees. The scent is so soft and soothing. Birds sing harmoniously and enjoy themselves in a perfectly sunny sky adorned with fluffy clouds. A stream of water murmurs its constant refrain as squirrels and rabbits play in the gardens. You breathe the sweet fragrance and enjoy this inspiring place.

You advance slowly, feeling the softness of the ground beneath your feet and breathing in the gentle perfumes. The sun warms your skin while nature plays to you a melody with a hint of a water stream, of singing birds and the whispering wind in the branches of the trees.

You go towards a wooden bench carved by nature in a huge tree trunk. You sit and enjoy the music of nature with your eyes closed, while the wind caresses your skin.

Suddenly, as if it were coming from deep within a large tree, a deep, calm voice is heard! "What do you desire?" "What do you want to be, have or do?"

Upon hearing these words, you open your eyes. You look all around you. Everything there is so perfect. You enjoy this precious time, inhaling the air. You feel so good. Everything is calm. You find yourself dreaming and imagining... Closing your eyes and detaching yourself, you let your imagination fly. You feel so good, so good...

Everything you can imagine and hope for can now materialize in this magical sky. You raise your gaze to the sky, and contemplate all that you want to have, in this magical sky. Everything you see has been created by your thoughts. You can now choose what you want and draw it into your life. It's for you! The Universe is benevolent and offers it to you.

You deserve it!

Whatever you desire, a new job, finding your soul mate, a new car, a reconciliation, a healthy body, an amount of money, a house, a trip, a friend... Let yourself dream. Create in your thoughts, that which you desire.

If you imagine yourself performing a certain task or doing something specific, you now do it with perfect ease. If you imagine being the person that you aspire to be, you are now this person who succeeds at everything she does with ease and success.

Simply let your imagination go. Let yourself be really carried away by your dreams... Everything is possible in your thoughts!

Once you have a new thought, it materializes immediately in the mysterious sky. You can attain everything that you want. Yes, you heard right, Everything, Everything, Everything !

Use all of your senses. Make this precious experience as real as possible, as if you were really living it.

When you see or feel the object or symbol of your desire floating in the sky, stretch your arms and grab what you want. It is yours now. Bring it close to your heart, hug it with passion and love it. You have attracted it. Keep it closely on your heart. Feel all of the emotions as you would, if you really had this thing in your life.

You are in a state of total satisfaction. Feel all the emotions that come with this sense of well-being. Feel them so strongly that all of your senses are mindful of these vibrations. Immerse your entire body in happiness. Breathe in the perfume of your desire. Touch its texture. Watch and absorb an image of your desire in three dimensions. Hear all the sounds and taste all the flavors that are part of situations where your wishes are fulfilled. Let your mind memorize all these wonderful feelings.

Your gratitude is total. You feel good and your whole body responds to this wonderful energy.

Take a few moments to clarify and create your dream to perfection. Savor these precious moments. You have what you want right here and right now. You really do, and it was so easy!

Savor your success. You are capable of being, having or doing whatever you want. Never forget that. Absolutely never forget that!

You feel so good!

Slowly return to the opening in the ceiling, stepping on the soft cool ground and quietly go down the stairs that take you back to your starting point. Go back to your original comfortable position and let your body and soul enjoy this sense of well-being.

When you feel ready, bring your mind back to the present moment. Gently open your eyes and move your body lightly.

You can practice this visualization as often as you like.

**YOU CAN ACTIVATE YOUR
ATTRACTION POWERS
BY CREATING FEELINGS
OF JOY AND WELL-BEING
THROUGH VISUALIZATION.**

You can also ask someone to read this text to you to really put you in the setting. We also offer on our website, a recording of this visualization that you can download to your computer or other electronic equipment. We have added sounds of nature that, for me, are very inspiring.

You can listen to this recording at your convenience. I like to use it at night before I go to sleep. This launches me on a good night's sleep since I generate vibrations of success which permeate my whole being. In addition to feeling good, my mind and body are positively conditioned and I benefit from this state of well-being while I sleep.

You can also change this visualization as you wish. My imaginative side often creates different visualizations. I love to leave this creative part of me surface. In this way you can also use your imagination to suit your own needs and your personality.

Above all, the most important is to have fun and feel good. Never forget that this is how you become a magnet that attracts what you want into your life.

So have fun!

☯ Recommended Actions

Practice this exercise as often as you wish.
You get emotionally closer to your goal this way.
Visit www.abundancethrunature.com
Some tools can help to
really put you in the required state
to attract what you want.

Chapter 17

Give, give and give again

*I*n order to receive, you must give.

There is a simple rule. You must give, if you want to receive. The Universe cannot deliver, if you do not give. We all have something to offer.

We all notice that when we smile at someone, people usually return our smile. It costs nothing to offer a smile, a recommendation, time, attention, a word of thanks, etc...

YOU HAVE TO GIVE
IN ORDER
TO RECEIVE.

You can brighten someone's day with a simple compliment. More people than you can imagine never receive kind words or encouragement in their lives. Yet, kind words are so easy to give. Just by paying a little attention to your neighbor, you can help create a better world. It is so refreshing to see someone's face light up when they receive a simple kind gesture or a kind word.

Also, few people sincerely express their thanks. A nice handwritten note often has a wonderful impact. Whoever receives it will appreciate this attention and will remember you in a very positive way.

I know that this is perhaps not valued enough, but to give up your seat on the bus to someone who is carrying a child, who has his arms full or who is older than you, is a nice practice.

When you wait in the checkout line of a store, you can also let someone who has fewer items than you, go ahead of you.

Such kindnesses are often the most appreciated.

Nature, meanwhile, has also a lot of beauty to offer us. Taking the time to watch a beautiful sunset with someone close to you can be a memorable moment. Receiving wildflowers picked spontaneously in a field, fills you with feelings of well-being.

GIVE, HOPING FOR NOTHING IN RETURN

Children very naturally know how to offer things freely: a big hug, a drawing, a small kindness. The child who brings home his magic rocks as a gift, always moves us.

As you can see, you can all offer something to someone today. Take the time to do it. Make it a constant practice. Give and give again

I am not only talking about money here. Sometimes money is what should be given in certain situations, but the abundance is not only money. You can find what you should be giving. In giving, we feel good and we send out vibrations to attract more abundance into our lives.

I dream of a world in which we would give more compliments and less criticism, give more smiles and less anger, give more recognition and less indifference, give more love and less hate...

With just a few changes in our habits, this is possible. Open the doors to abundance and happiness by getting into the habit of spreading and giving joy and love. The Universe will reward you in many ways.

Recommended Actions

Give today and tomorrow, again and again.
Abundance will knock on your door.

Chapter 18

To give and to receive, a balance

Giving is great, but so is receiving.

Many people think it is better to give and they have difficulty in receiving. It is all a question of balance. One is not better than the other.

You must learn to receive in order to have the life you dream of. The Universe always synchronizes events, people and a multitude of other elements so as to deliver what you attract into your life. Your duty is to be ready to accept them as they present themselves.

YOU MUST ACCEPT
EVEN THE SMALLEST THINGS
WITH JOY AND GRATITUDE

Most people don't know how to receive. Because they do not know how to receive, they don't receive what they want. Many have the feeling of not being worthy or deserving of it. This poor self-esteem usually comes from their childhood conditioning. Some develop the feeling of not being up to the standards of their peers or not meeting the expectations of others. There is also the feeling that sometimes we deserve to be punished. Since sometimes when you are older and there is no one to punish you, you unconsciously punish yourself.

Now remember that nothing has any meaning except the meaning that we give to it. You and only you can decide now to be worthy. If you decide it and state it, you are worthy. It is as simple as that.

When you reject the good things that the Universe wants to offer you, you cut off the flow of abundance. In other words, you send a message to the Universe that you do not want what is being presented to you or you are unworthy of it.

If a friend refused the gift that you offered out of the goodness of your heart, would you repeat this gesture by offering another gift? I don't think so and you would have good reason not to.

I once gave a gift to a friend for her birthday. A gift that I had chosen with joy and love just for her. She had helped me in one of my projects and I was pleased to offer this gift to her. She was not expecting it. After our meal, I handed her the present. She returned it to me, saying that it made her uncomfortable. I was so sad. This really disappointed me and we finished the evening a little coldly. Unknowingly, she had just denied me the pleasure of giving. I realized that it is very distasteful to be refused a gift which is given from the heart. Since I do not want others to feel this way, I receive gifts with joy and gratitude. I'm now pretty good at receiving and the Universe knows this.

It is all about energy. There must be a giver and a receiver.

Have you noticed that the rich are getting richer and the poor are getting poorer?

The rich have simply learned to receive and they do it with joy. If you are not ready to receive what the Universe wants to give you, your share will go to someone else. Probably to someone who has learned to receive. Don't say that this is unfair. The Law of Attraction is infallible. It delivers what you attract into your life.

Receive with gratitude and you will be like the rich people who receive in abundance.

Most people will not bend over to pick up a coin lying in the street. Me, I pick it up and I'm so happy! I am convinced that the Universe is sending me a message telling me that larger sums are on their way... But I have to accept, appreciate and be grateful for all the little things, so that the Universe understands that I am ready to receive.

I happened to see a friend throw her coins in the garbage when she was straightening out her desk drawers. For her, it was just small change. What message do you think she was sending to the Universe? As you can imagine, I have retrieved them. I also told her that I was willing to be her container for spare change that she wanted to throw away.

You also have to be watchful because you might get some good things in your life, but presented in a different way that you would have expected. Accept with gratitude all that is given to you. You may receive much more.

You must become an excellent receiver and a wonderful giver.

Everything in life is balanced!

☯ Recommended Actions
Be receptive to gifts from the Universe.
The Giving/Receiving balance is required.

Chapter 19

The images of my dreams

A picture is worth a thousand words and builds creative emotions.

I remember when I was little, I loved leafing through catalogs, magazines and newspapers to choose my Christmas gift. Then, I would cut out with my little scissors the picture of the new doll or the craft items that I wanted as a gift. I could then give my Christmas wish list to my parents. I showed them the picture to be sure I received exactly what I asked for. Sometimes it was different, but it was always better than what I had asked for.

I now understand that the Universe is like a good parent. I can ask for what I want. Then, I present it with images. It's so easy now with the Internet. We have such a wonderful selection of pictures to choose from.

I like to create a visualization dream board. I have installed one in front of my desk. I see it whenever I look up. I put all sorts of things on it. I also make small pictures arrangements.

For example, when I want to sell something, like a car, I take a picture of the car and put this notice above it: "Sold". In addition, if I want to replace this car with another one, I cut out pictures of the vehicle I want and I display them on my board, writing on them: "It's mine!"

When the wish I represented by an image is granted, I remove the picture from my "visualization dream board" and I put it in a box labeled "*Wish granted*". It is refreshing and energizing to look through this box content and realize that these images are things or situations that I attracted into my life.

IMAGES ALLOW US TO NURTURE OUR WISHES.

Since the child within me likes the pictures and we are now in the age of technology, I also now have a software that can run the video images of what I want. I add to them my affirmations as well as inspirational music. I run this video as often as I can and I let my subconscious register it all. Sometimes I dance to the rhythm of the music and say out loud my affirmations to the Universe.

I would like to propose to you to also try to use images of your desires on a consitant basis. Here are some examples.

- You can put these pictures in places where you will frequently see them.

- You can also put together a "wish scrapbook". It's so much fun to create. Just get a notebook, of any size or type.

Paste into it your photos, images, beautiful sayings, stickers and affirmations.

- Consider giving a beautifully decorated "wish scrapbook" as a gift. The person who receives it will be inspired to fill it with his or her personal dream images.

- You can also do as I do and get a "visualization dream board" that you can dress up with pictures of your dreams.

- If your desire is to travel, get a map and identify the places you want go with arrows or colorful pins.

- Make it a family or group project and let everyone add their images to the family or group "visualization dream board". It is exciting to know what others want, and perhaps we can also contribute to helping others realize their desire.

You simply have to make this process enjoyable, in your own way. It's a fun way to send messages about your desires to your subconscious and to the Universe. This also clearly defines what you want (including colors and all of the details).

☯ Recommended Actions

Use pictures of your desires
to motivate yourself. This also sends
clear messages to the Universe.

Chapter 20

Why abundance?

*L*ife is abundance! It is a reality that you can choose to envision.

Look around you. The air is in abundance. The leaves in the trees, plants, sand, drops of water from the rain or the sea, birds, snow... Everything is in abundance. I could make the list filling a book of all the things that are in abundance. It's everywhere around us.

All this abundance is offered to you by the Universe. Everything has been created for our highest good and for our pleasure. We should be so grateful.

The Law of Duality states that everything is dual. Here are some examples.

- Hot   Cold
- High   Low
- Day   Night
- Rich   Poor
- Healthy Sick

We have a choice of viewing the world in our own way, and this is often the result of our conditioning from childhood. The glass of water can be half empty or half full.

It is the same case for abundance or lack. Everything is perception. Everything has only the meaning that we give to it.

THE UNIVERSE OFFERS EVERYTHING TO US IN ABUNDANCE. LOOK AT NATURE...

Many refuse to accept abundance at several levels: health, love, money, success, happiness, etc. Sometimes, this is done unconsciously.

They think: "Why strive for abundance?" I'll try to answer this question in my own way.

I myself wish for abundance at all levels, simply because I am a creature of the Universe and we were created to live in abundance, like all creatures of nature.

I wish for health to live my life to the fullest, having wonderful experiences through the use of all my senses.

I want to be surrounded by love, because that's what everyone aspires to and life is so beautiful when we grow in love.

I want financial abundance so that I can be in a position to live my ideal life and help others do the same.

Some say that money does not buy happiness. However, I am sure it helps us to live to our full potential. And if I'm lucky enough to be able to generate a lot of money, I want to help others who are unable to do so. This will help to create a better world.

Money is a vehicle which allows us to show our gratitude to the Universe and also lets us allow others to benefit from it.

You can find your own reasons to attain abundance. If it motivates you and it is in harmony with the Universe, you are on the right path. So put this in writing while your inspiration is guiding you. When you clarify the reasons why you want to move towards abundance, you put your emotions into it and this displays the creative energy required to turn your desire into your reality.

☯ Recommended Actions

Find your personal reasons
that motivate you to achieve abundance, love,
health, wealth, freedom or any other desire.

Chapter 21

Play "As if..."

*C*reate your future by acting as if it is already happening.

In telling the story of when Kaïla was sick, I used this very powerful technique. With Vanessa, her big sister, we invented our imaginary world by pretending that Kaïla walked, sang and had fun with us in a perfectly normal way. It was so easy to play as if...

If you want to play "As If...", just get children involved. For them, it's so easy to do. They are full of imagination. It's a game they love!

**CHILDREN LOVE TO PLAY
"AS IF..."
BECOME INSPIRED
BY THEIR SPONTANEITY**

You can also motivate those around you to enter into your story and act as if...

Some people even organize theme nights on very motivational subjects, where everyone can play the role of a character they aspire to become. The theme may be, for example: "Who will I be in five years?" All the guests are instructed to dress and behave as the person they aspire to be. They must also join in the game with the other participants. Everyone must show to one another, that they believe and support the other people's dreams.

For example, if you wish to be a movie star, at this event you can talk about your latest movie that broke all the records. Discuss about scenes and other celebrities who shared this success with you. You can wear eccentric clothing and lots of jewelry (plastic jewelry works perfectly for such a disguise). It's all about playing the role.

Such evenings or activities that encourage your imagination through the use of this role play can spark very creative emotions. This energy can last within you a long time and act as a magnet to attract your desires to you.

Here, then, is the eighth step of the process that I suggest to you:

"Touch of nature" Creation Process

STEP 8:
Act as if your objective has already been realized.

Try to put yourself in the state of well-being that you would be in, if your desire was achieved. It's magical and it's fun.

This forces you to really experience your anticipated feelings. It's very exciting to know that we can make our scenario the most beautiful and perfect as possible, just as we want.

When you are enjoying nature, you constantly play an "As if...." game. And you are enjoying it. You project the elements into the future.

Let's share some examples:

- When the first flower buds show their presence, you intuitively think. *It's going to be so beautiful when the flowers bloom. I can already smell their perfume.* You are already appreciating the beauty of the flowers that are coming. You act "As if...." the flowers have already bloomed.

- When rain showers stop and a rainbow points to the horizon, you look already forward to your next activity prepared to enjoy the sun. Even before the sky has cleared, you act "As if...." the sun was already there.

- When a young baby starts to crawl on the floor, you are already getting ready for his first steps. You help him stand up, you buy shoes for him. You act "As if...." he is already walking.

Such examples abound in nature. Note that you never doubt what you want to see happen. You have confidence in the Universe. You do not say:

- Can the flowers bloom?

- Will the sun shine again?

- Will this child be able to walk?

You must put yourself in this same state in order to attract what you want to you. Act "As if...." it was already your reality and it will become this new reality.

☯ Recommended Actions
Find opportunities to enhance
your future life scenarios by playing
"As if..." and having fun doing it.

Chapter 22

Love produces miracles

*S*end out love and your life will be magically transformed.

Most of all, **love yourself**. Feel deep love for yourself. You must love yourself to attract abundance.

Have you ever noticed that when you're in love, your whole world seems so beautiful. You have energy and you feel you can achieve the impossible. It is such a powerful energy.

Remember a time when you felt your heart sing, vibrating with love. Perhaps it is for the person who shares your life, or for your children, your family or your pet. For me, I think back to the time when I held one of my daughters in my arms when she was a baby. I felt this for each of my wonderful daughters. I looked at her and my heart was filled with love. I was so filled with love that I conveyed this love to her and everyone around me.

I like to bring myself to this state where my heart is filled with love and I send this love to the whole world by saying to myself, *"I love you, I love you, I love you"*. It is sometimes so strong that it sends chills through my body. Everyone can feel different emotions in different ways. We are all different.

I also send out this powerful love to those I would call "challenges" in my life. Indeed, it is in hoping for the best for all (even those who bring challenges into your life) that we attract what is best in our own lives.

Love and bless your "challenges" because this will dissolve all negativity.

ALL THE LOVE AND BLESSINGS THAT YOU SEND OUT WILL COME BACK TO YOU MULTIPLIED.

If you despise and wish bad things for those messengers who bring challenges to your life, this is what you will attract into your own life.

In the morning, I like to say this little prayer by sending love as a light wind all around the earth (in my imagination, of course):

> *"I wish for all men (including women and children), peace, love, joy, happiness, health, prosperity, abundance, freedom and all the blessings of God."*

The author Joe Vitale proposes in his book "Zero Limits", a method called Ho'oponopono, which comes from Dr. Hew Len of Hawaï. Through this method, Dr.

Len cured all the psychiatric patients in a penitentiary center, without ever having met any of the patients in person.

This method is based on love and frees our bodies, souls or minds from any problems. It is summed up in four affirmations that you repeat in succession, aloud or in your head:

These sentences are:

"I love you"
"I am sorry"
"Please forgive me"
"Thank you"

This Ho'oponopono method consists in taking and assuming full responsibility for our lives. This method states that we create our life, so we are no longer victims. In this way, we enter a state of love and acceptance.

When a problem arises, we are used to accuse someone or something else. We look outside ourselves for the origin of the problem. What occurs in our external world can exist only if it is conceived in thought in our minds, in our inner world. Since we are all interconnected, when a person solves an undesirable situation with the Ho'oponopono method, everyone around him benefits of it.

We must accept what is part of the problem or who is more or less connected to it, to begin to heal the problem that lies within us. By cleansing the problem within ourselves, we change the external situation. Through the phrases of the Ho'oponopono method, you ask the Universe to cleanse and purify the source of the problems which are memories. No need to relive any pain or to know where it originates.

If you are not comfortable with all of the phrases, you can say only those you want. Simply by constantly repeating *"I love you"*, you can obtain remarkable results. Try repeating this phrase in your head all day.

You'll be amazed. I'm not saying it's easy to do, but if you do it often enough, you will get into the habit. You'll feel good because your mind is occupied with thoughts of love. You will see that you will vibrate in a very positive way and you will attract such positive things to yourself.

Imagine for a moment a world in which everyone sends love to everyone and everything. What a wonderful world that would be...

LOVE
IS THE MOST POWERFUL
CREATIVE ENERGY

We would all benefit from experiencing and emitting the greatest possible love for everything around us.

The more love we vibrate, the more quickly we attract that which we desire into our lives. With love, we are on the most creative frequency.

Love is in some ways, the magic wand that can make all of your desires materialize. I love knowing that I have the ability to articulate this magic wand. We all have this privilege within us and it comes from our heart.

☯ Recommended Actions

Learn to put yourself in a
state in which you are vibrating with love.
Repeat *"I love you"* until this
becomes an habit.
You will transform into a magnet of love.

Chapter 23

Our limiting beliefs

Your present beliefs have created your present life.

In order to pass onto or move up to a higher level of success, you must change some of your current beliefs that are limiting your current level of achievement. To change your reality, you must change your thoughts.

We all have a different **plan for success**. It is this **plan for success** that is responsible for your present life. To change your life, just change your **plan for success**. This is just what I am going to help you to do. We will use proven methods that people who excel, apply in their lives.

**YOUR CURRENT
PLAN FOR SUCCESS
HAS GIVEN YOU
YOUR CURRENT RESULTS.
CHANGE IT AND
YOU WILL CHANGE
YOUR RESULTS AND YOUR LIFE.**

To begin, you must make a serious examination of your beliefs if you want to change your life and your results. For me, when I examined my personal beliefs, I realized what I wanted, but this often brought up strong emotions. Especially the fear of not succeeding. When I was in this spiral of negative emotions, I ended up not believing that change was possible for me. But I used some tips that I will share with you so that you can use them too. You will see, this can change a life!

During your journey to abundance, you must change some of your limiting beliefs in order to change your reality. To achieve these changes, I propose a very simple method. To do this exercise, use two different color pens. The dark color is used for the negative stuff (items 1 to 3). The red color is used for the new belief (item 4). This red color enhances what you desire.

1. **Awareness**: Analyze what you have heard, what you have seen or what you have experienced about abundance, health, love, success or money since your childhood. Note all your observations. This may stir up emotions inside of you.

2. **Understanding**: Think about the impact that this has had on your life. What has any such beliefs brought to or materialized in your life? Write everything that comes to mind.

3. **Dissociation**: Realize, that some of these beliefs are not beliefs that you really want to hold. These limiting

beliefs have sometimes created quite the opposite of what you wanted in your life. Now you have the choice to believe and think in a new, more positive way. Reject those beliefs that you no longer want.

4. **Your new belief:** Now, using the red color pen, define a new affirmation that will help develop your full potential. You can write a new affirmation for each negative belief you have. Note everything that comes to mind. When your new empowering belief is written in red, use your dark color pen and scratch with a line over your initial limiting belief.

5. **Fix these new beliefs into your consciousness through repetition.** Say them, listen to them, sing them, and above all, believe them with your whole being. Several tools for fixing new beliefs in your mind are available. For example, when you want to fix your new belief in your mind, you can play the same music while you state conviction, your new affirmation. You can also use a particular odor (ex: coffee, flower...). Then you will automatically associate the music or the odor with your new belief. Many other techniques are also available, but I cannot cover them all in this manual.

Once your limiting belief is replaced by a more constructive one, your reality will change very rapidly.

For example, here are some negative beliefs that I have replaced with much more positive beliefs. You can create your own list.

Negative: I have to work hard to make money.

Positive: By living a balanced life, I easily attract abundance and money.

a. Negative: We cannot live from our passion.

Positive: I do what I love and what excites me and the Universe always provides for my needs and more.

b. Negative: It is normal to gain weight as we age.

Positive: With my healthy choices, I maintain my weight.

Nature is always changing. When a seed falls to the ground, it does not question whether the environment has all the nutrients for it to grow. It takes root and grows as it can and depends on its environment. In general, all the elements of nature are harmonious with each other. The Universe is abundant and we all have access to this abundance. It is important to avoid restricting ourselves with our limiting beliefs.

You can have, be and do everything that you want.

☯ Recommended Actions

Any limiting belief can be replaced with a constructive belief and love. Change your negative beliefs and experience a better reality.

Chapter 24

What can I do for you?

*C*ontribute to the success of others and you will attain success yourself.

The Universe feels the energy that you release. By wanting something too much, by saying that you need it or by putting yourself in this state of need, sometimes your energy ends up driving back the realization of your desires rather than attracting them.

To realign yourself and neutralize the energy, direct your attention on another subject.

Try to develop the habit of helping others succeed or rejoicing in their victories. By helping your fellowman, you release a powerful energy. Also, since you attract what you release, the Universe sets everything in motion to help you to achieve your own wishes.

In our society, which is focused on performance and competition, it's everyone for himself. This mentality comes from the fact that people believe that there are not enough customers, contracts, food, doctors, money or other things for everyone. So they try to attract to   themselves the most customers, contracts, food, doctors or money.

THE UNIVERSE WILL REWARD YOU
ACCORDING TO
THE HELP THAT
YOU GIVE TO THE
GREATEST NUMBER OF PEOPLE

As I have already explained, the Universe is abundant. With our limiting beliefs, we attract everything in a limited way, because it is our thoughts that release the energy of limitation.

Offer your help to someone. Ask *"What can I do for you?"*. Sometimes, someone may need advice, a sympathetic ear, a small favor, the name of someone you can refer to them...

The people you help are usually very grateful. As for yourself, you will feel good and your energy will be able to attract even more creative events in your life. Isn't that rewarding?

When I was little, at one point we lived near a farm. As on most agricultural property, there was an adorable black and white dog. This dog used to round up the cows from the pasture to bring them back to the barn. He was very intelligent. One day a young calf was injured. He had bled all night. The dog stayed by his side to protect it and to give it comfort. At dawn, when the rescuers arrived, he would not leave the calf. It is fascinating how animals have this instinct to protect the weakest. This is done intuitively. A dog, living a good relationship with his master, will sacrifice his life to protect his master.

146

We are also blessed with marvelous instincts, with the added bonus of intelligence and varying emotions. With all these advantages, we should be able to find a wide range of ways to help our fellowman.

I like to think that animals are wonderful messengers who teach us by example.

One of the keys to success is **service to others**.

We all have talents, knowledge, contacts or tools that we can offer to others. We are all unique and we can share our authenticity.

You enjoy being helped. It's just the same for others. Help as often as you can.

☯ Recommended Actions

Try to help as many people as possible
and the Universe in return
will help you achieve your own desires.

Chapter 25

Action is required

*T*ake action to activate the Law of Attraction.

To have a great crop of tomatoes, you must first plant the seeds in the ground. Without this first action you will never reap any tomatoes.

To ensure a quality crop, you can also do several other things, such as: watering when needed, applying fertilizer, weeding, etc.

YOU WILL ACHIEVE RESULTS BY THE CHOICES YOU MAKE AND THE ACTIONS YOU TAKE.

Too many people spend a great part of their precious time watching TV. Some TV programming can be empowering and interesting. However, these long hours of inactivity lets your brain soak up information that is not always creative. This precious time can be used to create your dream life.

It is disturbing to see all these people who watch the weekly broadcasts so diligently. They are watching others living their lives... It's up to you to decide now the future that you want. Stop watching others live the life that you dream of and create your own reality by living your life to the fullest.

Each day that goes by will never return. You should enjoy your life now! Do not waste all those precious moments that you will never see again. You have so much to offer to the world. Each of us is unique and we all possess treasures that should be shared with the world.

Here is the ninth step in the process that I propose:

"Touch of nature" Creation Process

STEP 9:
Take action to achieve
your intentions (desires).

Once you have the inspiration to do something, just do it. Do not wait until your energy disappears. When you have an inspiration, the energy to achieve it always comes with it. Take advantage of this exciting energy.

You do not have to see in advance the entire road that you have to follow in order to achieve your desire. Have faith in the Universe. The actions you need to take will eventually be revealed, one after the other.

It's like a road on which you cannot see your destination. The road is revealed to you as you go down it. You trust that even if you do not see the final destination, you'll get there by following the road.

It's the same for your dreams and desires. Your actions bring you closer to your goal. Have confidence.

Sometimes, the Universe may delay the realization of your desire. It always depends on whether you're ready to receive. You may sometimes believe you are ready, but the Universe may choose, for your highest good, to delay this realization. The Universe may even grant your desires in another form or color that differ from what you wanted.

Sometimes, a single action is required and the Universe delivers to you what you want. However, there will be situations where you have to take continuous actions. When you perform your actions and demonstrate a commitment to achieving your goal, the Universe will do its part. It will organize and synchronize events, situations and meetings to support and promote your desires.

The Universe is all powerful and loves you!

Show by your actions, your willingness to have, do and be what you want and the Universe will assist you!

Recommended Actions
Make a habit of taking action.
Always take steps in
the direction of your dreams.

Chapter 26

Positive thinking spiral

A positive thinking spiral acts like a hurricane on negativity.

I will show you a way of thinking that I learned in Mindy Audlin's book, "What If It All Goes Right?" It is one of the little tricks that I apply in my life.

When we are in uncertain situations, we are in the habit of imagining the worst. Have you already done this? This is how our society works and so we have learned it as well. Our way of thinking is imbued in us since childhood, and so it is normal that we are conditioned this way. But is this kind of thinking really to our advantage?

Let's take an example:

1. My neighbors had a bad flu and I heard on the news that cases of the flu were on the increase.

   Here is the usual way of thinking, in a **negative thinking spiral**:

   - What if the neighbor's children already have the virus and then they give it to our children…

- What if our children get the flu, it's clear that the whole family will be infected in no time...

- What if before the symptoms appear, we contaminate the people in the office...

- What if then, they also contaminate their families...

- What if the cases are so numerous that hospitals do not have the manpower to take care of everyone...

- What if it was like with the last bad flu that killed so many people...

- What if, what if, what if...

Do you recognize what you are hearing? What do you think such thoughts attract? There is no doubt, these thoughts in this example attract the flu!

This form of negative thinking spiral usually happens when you think about something you are not happy about, and the more you think of it, the worst it seems. These thoughts could be about an existing situation, something you fear or something you invent or assume that might occur in the future. These assumed thoughts about the future attract another that is also invented but which is not usually based on any event. Each of these thoughts amplifies the negative version of this purely invented scenario. It is a very powerful form of thinking. But, as you may have noticed, it is not positive at all. By imagining the worst, with the words:

"*What if...*", it opens the door to endless scenarios, each one more chilling than the others.

This way of thinking attracts nothing positive in your life. The medias use this form of advertising a lot to attract the attention of the public. And since so many people subscribe to this way of thinking, it is exactly what the vast majority of the people attract.

Now let's move on to the positive side, thinking through the positive thinking spiral. Let's use the same example.

2. My neighbors had a bad flu and I heard on the news that cases of the flu were on the increase.

Here is the **positive thinking spiral**, a new way of seeing things:

- What if this flu could finally allow them to take time to relax a bit...

- What if once relaxed, they become closer to one another...

- What if this quiet period was just what they needed to read the inspirational book that we gave them for Christmas...

- What if our neighbors realized that they could finally take more time to do what they want and love in life...

- What if it was the perfect time for them to make the changes they have wanted to make for a long time…

- What if this flu was just the beginning of a period of positive changes in their lives…

This version of the situation is completely different and so much more energizing. For each hardship, we can always find positive.

This form of **positive thinking spiral** consists of a first positive thought that attracts another. We imagine the best scenario in a given situation and we enhance it. It goes on in this way to improve the scenario. It is a very powerful form of thinking.

BY IMAGINING WHAT COULD BE
THE BEST
IN EVERY SITUATION
WE OPEN THE DOOR TO AN
INFINITE NUMBER OF SCENARIOS,
ONE MORE ENERGIZING
THAN THE OTHERS

You need to motivate yourself to think in this new positive way and to make it into a habit. At first, it is more difficult because our society is not conditioned to think in this manner. The more you practice it, the more you can create positive situations. With this mindset, you will emit very positive vibrations and that is what you will attract. All positive things!

Recommended Actions

Practice the positive thinking spiral.
Create your own energizing scenarios.
Develop this way of thinking and
watch your life become transformed
in a positive way.

Chapter 27

The power of detachment

*C*elebrate your freedom. Free yourself from your ties...

Life and nature are filled with stories of love and detachment. As humans, we have children, knowing fully that we have to let them grow up, live their own experiences and make their own choices. We cannot keep them close to us forever, no matter how much we love them. You have to let them fly away with their own wings.

When there is no detachment, energy becomes paralyzing.

Once you understand that you are loved, that the Universe is benevolent and that it is always there to support you, you do not feel the need to hold on to people, things or experiences.

When we are strongly attached to a harmful situation, our powers are limited. We cut ourselves off from our inner powers of creation. Have faith in the Universe.

You can always express your feelings without hurting anyone. Be diplomatic. Be as considerate towards others as you would want others to be with you.

Take a step back and examine your situation. Let your mind and body relax. Your brain will recover its creative powers. Stay focused on solutions. Ask the Universe for help.

To live in harmony, we must accept differences. Many of our disappointments are caused by our expectations. We cannot control everything.

Let the joy and happiness you dream of, guide your thoughts and actions.

Too many people strongly cling to lawsuits, breakdowns, failures, death or other disturbing events. They talk about them and negative emotions are constantly emitted from their comments. They are not aware of it, but they create their own ball and chain that immobilizes them. Such energies are extremely harmful to one's health and for one's future experiences. Under such conditions, they should let go, in order to release old beliefs and realize that those old beliefs do not serve them anymore.

Put your worries, your fears and your limitations in the hands of the Universe and focus on what is good for you. Let go of the negative energy within you.

Here is the tenth step in the process that I propose:

"**Touch of nature**" **Creation Process**

STEP 10:
Detach yourself
from results,
let go.

In my story of when Kaïla was sick, when I entrusted my child to St. Anne, I did not realize at the time that I had activated the powers of detachment. I did not understand this until later when looking back on the situation. Without being aware, I had sent a message to the Universe that I had faith in it and I believed that the powers of the Universe would comfort me and ease my pain.

The Universe has delivered so much more than I expected. It gave me an energizing force and bathed me in this benevolent light. The Universe has also fulfilled all my dreams by healing my little Kaïla. I realized that detachment is incredibly powerful and that for the Universe nothing is impossible.

I sincerely wish each of you could experience such a blessing.

☯ Recommended Actions

Let go, exhibit detachment.
The Universe will deliver the best
it has for you.

Chapter 28

Make room

*T*he Universe hates emptiness. It fills empty spaces.

To attract the positive into your life, you must leave room for everything that you want to come to you!

Have you noticed how the Universe is capable of filling every space of fertile land with vegetation? It fills the sea, the land and our skies with creatures perfectly fit for them, one more beautiful than another.

The Universe is constantly creating. It brings ideas to a calm mind that is willing to receive. It knows exactly how to fill each space.

Do your housekeeping. It feels so nice to be in a tidy office or home. It is the same for your body. You can free yourself from your tensions by realigning yourself with what is good for you.

Empty your closets of things that you have not worn for years, organize your files and your garage, clean out your dressers and your storage space. You'll feel so light.

Naturally, this requires energy, but the energy you feel will be greater and more peaceful once you have completed these tasks. You will release an energy that was dormant in you. Stop putting these things off. Begin drawer by drawer, closet by closet, room by room and you'll be finished sooner than you think. You may even surprise yourself by doing it with enthusiasm.

THE UNIVERSE ALWAYS FILLS EMPTY SPACES

By doing this, you show the Universe that you are ready to welcome good things into your life and that you even made the required space for them. Since the Universe does not like empty spaces and since you are releasing positive energy, it will put everything in place for you to get what you want.

It is not important for you to know how these things will come to you. The Universe takes care of these details. You must have faith! You do not need to provide money to buy these things. If it has to come to you through a purchase, you will have the money to buy it.

All the things you want to get rid of can be sold at a garage sale or some other way. They can also be given to charitable organizations or to those in need. You'd be surprised how many people appreciate, as if they were treasures, what you want to get rid of.

164

It is important to add that it is preferable not to use the money raised in this way to spend on useless treats. You need to show the Universe that you are serious in your approach to achieve your dreams and you have complete faith. You can use the money to pay debts, invest in a financial freedom fund or in any investment that earns a profit.

In addition, for example, if you want to meet the right person with whom you can share your life, try to make room around you for the personal belongings of that person. Make room and visualize this future person's clothing in your closet and all around. This sends a clear message to the Universe that you are ready to welcome this person into your life.

If you need furniture for your living room, make room for it now and imagine yourself touching and enjoying it and also seeing exactly as it would be placed.

If you want a new vehicle, go try out the model you prefer. Soak up the smell, touch the textures, look at and remember every detail, hear the noise of the engine and of the radio and feel all the joy that flows through your body during the test drive. When you return home, make sure there is a present or future parking spot for this new vehicle. When you leave your home, look at that parking space, imagining your next vehicle in that space... patiently waiting for you.

Invent your scenarios, go through them depending on what you want. The Universe will fill the void, just as nature fills the spaces of fertile soil with vegetation.

☯ Recommended Actions

Make room for what you want in your life.
Get rid of anything that is stagnating around you.
The Universe will fill that void.

Chapter 29

Neutralize negative energy

*I*t is wise to leave a tense situation.

We all know that anger is a negative energy. There is a wide variety of negative emotions. To further explain, I'll use the example of anger as a negative emotion.

Some people cannot control their anger or certain negative emotions. We've all heard stories about people who commit crimes under the influence of great anger or uncontrolled negative emotions. Anger often begins with a trigger event or arguments that become more intense. In these cases, each of the parties wants to be right.

Actually, always wanting to be right carries a certain price.

We all know people who are always right. Only their opinions count. Their whole life is centered on the fact of always being right. Are they happy, wealthy and healthy?

I prefer to feel good and attract abundance than to be right, unhappy, poor or sick.

In some situations, it is useless to continue the argument, because often, under the tension and negative energy, each of the parties has a limited view of the situation. In other words, each sees only his own version and perspective of things. In tense situations, it is rare that the people involved will be able to find a solution.

If we wish to take control of our lives and attract what we desire, it is important to minimize and even eliminate these bad energies from our lives. Since they attract no good, why keep these bad energies around us? Remember that to attract what you want, you must feel good. No one feels good in a climate of anger or hostility.

At a seminar I attended, I learned about a study that was performed on several subjects to evaluate the power of anger. Anger, even without words, but with the emotion linked to anger, can kill a hamster! Indeed, the anger of a single minute produces toxic gases that are released through the mouth, nose, and the body of the angry subject. These gases are sufficient to kill a hamster. Wow! This is pretty upsetting!

One minute of anger can kill a hamster!

In addition, anger that lasts a few more minutes can kill a guinea pig. The worst part is that the study states that the angry subject inhales the gas products. These gases are very harmful to health and cause sickness. The angry person believes that by getting angry at someone, he sends negative energy to that person and by doing so it would be logical to believe that the other person receives all of the adverse effects of the anger. Well, this is not the case...

It is the angry person who inhales toxic gases that make him sick, and who receives and releases negative energy and attracts even more negativity into his life! It is the Law of Attraction at work... All that you send out comes back to you. This person will hurt himself. Often, simply to have the satisfaction of being right. Naturally, the other person reaps some of the negative effects, but it is the angry person who receives the biggest harvest of negative energies.

When you are in a situation where someone insists on being right, be smart... and withdraw from the argument and let the tension go. If the arguer has no one with whom to continue his arguments, he will automatically calm down. The situation will be more favorable to finding a solution. If the situation persists, go somewhere else. Find something to do.

WE MAINTAIN OUR POSITIVE ENERGY BY AVOIDING STRESSFUL SITUATIONS.

However, sometimes we have to face certain situations which may be some greater challenges for us. We cannot and must not evade our responsibilities.

At home, when someone starts to get angry, another person always says something like "*Be careful not to kill a hamster*". When anger is more intense, it is something like "*Beware of the dogs, negative energy is around...*". It makes us smile and it reduces the tension.

By educating those around you to the harmful effects of anger, you can help each other by remembering the story of the hamster. Attention is then released to a more joyful topic.

Everyone prefers to live in a peaceful and energizing atmosphere. Everyone can then vibrate positively. By contributing, each in our own way to minimize the amplitude and frequency of negative energy, we create a better and calmer world where we can live well and evolve.

☯ Recommended Actions

Remember the story of the hamster.
You should avoid and separate yourself from stressful situations.
Seek a calm and energizing atmosphere.

Chapter 30

How to create?

You are the creator of your life.

We are beings with amazing powers. We are on earth to have our own experiences and evolve. We are living beings, just like all things in nature, but we have an extraordinary asset, the power of thought that creates our reality.

I like to compare our evolution to the life of a tree. Each tree is unique and perfect in itself. It is programmed to adapt, develop and reach its full potential. It exists to fill a need in the life cycle created by the Universe.

The tree begins with a seed which has all of its DNA in it. If it is destined to be an oak, it cannot become a pine. Before breaking through to the world, it develops its roots and finds everything it needs to create balance in order to become strong. When its roots are sufficiently developed, it releases its small stalk through the earth. It then draws on its nourishment and its forces from the elements of nature, such as water, soil, sun, the coolness of the night and on the environment that surrounds it.

In order to grow stronger, the tree needs to strengthen its roots. Each stage of its growth that can be seen above the ground is always preceded by a constant strengthening of its roots. It constantly grows and changes. Strong roots produce good fruit. To improve the quality of fruit you should always improve the quality of the roots with fertilizer, nutrients or whatever is needed.

When the tree ceases to evolve, it begins to wither and die. If a tree does not evolve, it dies and becomes transformed. This is true for any element in nature.

Let's compare this with our evolution.

Each human being is unique and perfect in itself. He is programmed to adapt, develop and reach his full potential. He exists to fill a need in the life cycle created by the Universe.

The human being begins with a cell which has his DNA in it. Before breaking through to the world, he develops his beliefs and finds everything he needs to create balance in order to become strong. When his beliefs are strong enough, the human being will release his potential and his authenticity. He will draw all his energy and forces from the elements of nature, from his spiritual dimension, his parents, his teachers, the media and his surrounding environment.

In order to grow stronger, the human being needs to strengthen his beliefs. Each stage of his growth and change is preceded by a constant strengthening of his beliefs. He constantly grows and evolves. The choices of his beliefs dictate the outcome. Strong beliefs produce good outcomes.

TO CHANGE THE QUALITY OF YOUR OUTCOMES YOU ALWAYS HAVE TO CHANGE THE QUALITY OF YOUR BELIEFS

To evolve and move to a higher level and improve outcomes, the human being beforehand must always change and improve his beliefs. When the human being ceases to evolve, he begins to wither and die. If man does not change, no longer learns and ultimately, remains stagnant, then he, like the tree, will die and become transformed.

To put it another way, if you dislike your current outcomes (your weight, your love life, your career, your finances...), you must change and strengthen your beliefs. Remember, your current beliefs have created your current life and the experiences you are living now and in the near future.

Just as to change the quality of fruit produced by a tree, the roots must be strengthened, it is the same for us humans. Change your beliefs and your outcomes, as well as your whole life, will change.

You can decide here and now to continue to live your life following the currents that carry you along, or you can decide to take control of your life and have, be and do what you want.

We were all brought onto this earth to live our full potential by experiencing and testing our creative powers.

**EVERYTHING IS POSSIBLE.
CREATE YOUR DREAMS
WITH YOUR THOUGHTS
AND POWERFUL EMOTIONS.
THE KEY THAT ALLOWS YOU
TO ACCESS
THE FUTURE YOU DREAM OF
IS IN YOUR MIND.**

Here are all the steps in the **Creation Process** that I propose. These are the steps that I have applied intuitively in my life and that have delivered and still deliver wonderful results. I was inspired to follow these steps. An indescribable force guides me. It guides all of us. You just have to know how to listen.

Adopt the following **Creation Process** and I can assure you that your life will transform itself in the most unexpected and admirable way. Everything is in your brain. It is true that you have to make some effort. But isn't your dreamed life worth it? Do not forget that this Creation Process becomes easier, as you use it.

Here are the steps in the Creation Process:

"Touch of nature" Creation Process

1) Be grateful for everything that is beautiful and good.

2) State what you no longer want.

3) Define what you do want.
   (I want – Why?)

4) Outline your intention (your desire) and put it in writing.

5) Formulate affirmations that support your intentions (desires).

6) Believe with certainty that it is possible.

7) Visualize your life with your intentions realized.

8) Act as if your intention has already been realized.

9) Take action to achieve your intentions (desires).

10) Detach yourself from outcomes, let go.

All of these steps are very simple. The formula is not complicated. The secret lies in the **energy that you put into practice.**

You must use this Creation Process as something easy. Do it to have fun with your family and friends. This Creation Process is so fun, natural and easy. Just decide you will be having fun attracting everything you want. And guess what, this is exactly what will happen.

EVERYTHING IS A QUESTION OF ENERGY (OF FEELING)

Quantum science now shows that our thoughts, our feelings and our energies create and change matter. This is not something unreal or imaginary. This is true, and now proven by science. Many experiments have been conducted on this topic.

Society is starting to open up to this new reality. We do, however, have embryonic knowledge of the Law of Attraction. Just as, at one time, everyone believed that the earth was flat and then it was proved it was round, today we are discovering that we are creators. We do not yet know how to maximize our power of creation so as to reach our full potential.

I continue to apply the steps in this Creation process that I am proposing for you. By doing so, I am realizing my dreams. This process works very well with the level of knowledge that I currently have.

176

I am passionate about everything related to our personal growth and I am always learning about it. I experiment with my own experiences. I am having fun and realizing my dream life.

In the near future, probably sooner than we think, perhaps we will find new methods that are as powerful as a magic wand.

I hope so ... Wow!
How much fun would that be!

Recommended Actions

Apply the steps of the
"Touch of nature" Creation process
Do them with conviction and by applying
your wonderful energy.
You will realize your dreams.

Chapter 31

Focus on solutions

*S*olutions give us energy.

Happy people are not people who do not have problems, they are simply people who focus on solutions.

Consider this fact. It is so powerful. While you are thinking, going back and reliving the problem, you magnify it and let it guide you through this situation. You become a victim. You go in circles and attract nothing but problems and still more problems.

You have the power at any time to take control of your thoughts. You can do it as fast as a snap of the fingers. All you have to do is focus your attention on solutions. That is something that is so much more constructive. There is always one or more solutions to every problem.

**WHEN YOU EXPERIENCE A PROBLEM,
DIRECT YOUR ATTENTION
TOWARDS THE SOLUTIONS.
IT IS ALWAYS
MORE ENERGIZING.**

You can ask yourself "*What can I do to fix this problem?*". Solutions, images and clues will flood your mind. Stay calm and coldly analyze the possibilities. Deep inside you, you know the best solution for solving your problem.

As you evaluate and consider the solutions, you will divert your attention away from the problem. This is really important. This way you open the door to new possibilities.

Sometimes you may feel the need to consult with someone to clarify your choice or simply to help you analyze your various options. A real friend or someone who knows you well can provide support to you. But, above all, avoid talking to someone who has a negative nature. Be selective about the people you trust.

I think we unconsciously generate problems in order to enable ourselves to evolve. Perhaps life presents you with challenging situations in various forms. You must resolve these situations and/or find a way to adapt. It is important however, that your challenges are not the same as those that you have already encountered. Because if they are always the same, it means that you have not changed or that you have not resolved issues that you should have resolved.

We must solve the problem once and for all and move on to other things. This is how we evolve.

**IF A PROBLEM SEEMS IMMENSE,
IT IS BECAUSE
WE FEEL SMALLER
THAN THE PROBLEM.
WE MUST EVOLVE IN ORDER TO
FEEL BIGGER
THAN OUR PROBLEMS.**

Let's take an example:

You drive to your appointment to meet with a new customer. You have organized things well and written down the directions to follow. Suddenly, the traffic is diverted because of an accident on the road. Because of this detour, you miss the road you should have taken according to the direction you wrote down. You can become agitated and imagine that you will be late, but this will not solve the situation. You say the story over and over again and tell yourself that this only could happen to you or that it is always the same. With this kind of thinking, it's guaranteed that you will arrive late... if you arrive at all. If you continue to think that you are really unlucky and you continue to brood over the problem when you arrive at the client's office, it is obvious that your meeting cannot be productive. How could it be different? You are simply vibrating in the *"problem attraction"* mode.

Instead, consider solutions... If you no longer know where to go, find a place to stop and ask someone to help you. People are usually very happy to help you. You can always find a way to reach your destination with a smile, confident and positive. With this attitude, your meeting has a better chance of being productive and ending in a positive way.

It is all in your attitude. You can now decide to join the group of happy people who choose to see problems but to focus on solutions. It's a way of life that you can develop with practice. This is how we evolve!

☯ Recommended Actions

Make the choice that allows you to evolve
and to progress in life.
Focus your attention on solutions
instead of problems.

Chapter 32

My desires are my secrets

*E*veryone has the right to his or her secret garden.

In order to create, some say you should tell others what you want manifested. They think this allows for the desired situation to be stimulated. Act as if it were true, so that it all happens faster. It's one way of seeing things...

This may work for some, but I prefer to maintain my little secret garden in many situations. What I ask of the Universe, in writing or spontaneously, is very personal.

When I ask for something, I **believe** that I can have it. My conviction and my determination are very strong and I have a clear vision of my desire already realized. And so, I send creative vibrations to the Universe.

I play with my ideas and I question things. Sometimes, I change my mind during the process of creation. I have the right, since these are my thoughts, my desires. I don't have to justify my thoughts and my inspirations. I believe I am the creator of my life!

When I tell people what I want to create or have manifested, most are skeptical. Some people start to criticize, to try to convince me that it's impossible or to think that I am out of my head. I must then try to convince or reassure them. This lowers my energy and makes me doubt. I don't have to waste my energy justifying what I want to create.

So now I create, using the angels and the forces of the Universe, by simply using the steps of my Creation Process.

Sometimes, I can juggle and write for a number of days in a row about a particular request. I ask questions. This technique works really well.

ASK THE UNIVERSE CLEARLY
AND BELIEVE
THAT YOU HAVE ALREADY
RECEIVED.

Here is an example of a situation that happened in my life.

At one time in my life, my husband and I suggested to my father-in-law that we buy his home and convert it to a bi-generational house. This would allow him to stay with us, but have his own apartment attached to the house. He enjoyed and accepted the idea.

We drew up the blueprints and presented the project. My father-in-law was thrilled and he would talk enthusiastically about his future home. We did not sign a contract of sales document because he said that he would take care of that later.

We put up our family home for sale and it sold very quickly. We negotiated a few months before moving out of the house. When we asked my stepfather to finalize the purchase of his house so we could begin renovation work, he told us he was not ready. He wanted to keep his house. He apologized. He had changed his mind.

Wow, that was really unexpected! We had no home and we had to find a place to relocate our family of five children. We started looking for a new house and made many offers of purchase. Nothing worked. Finally we rented a house and continued our search for a new home. After a few months, the owner of the house we were living in temporarily needed his home...

Once more, we moved and lived in the house of a friend who had it up for sale. Naturally, should the house be sold, we would have to vacate the premises immediately. This was becoming a habit...

This was a very difficult period. Sylvain and I worked full-time. In addition, I had to be at our equestrian center on weekends and in the evening. We had no relief and these moves exhausted me. Especially since Megan, our youngest daughter, was still on the bottle.

All the responsibilities related to my government job, our start-up enterprise (the equestrian center), our young children, the lack of a home and the constant tension of having to be forced to move with little notice, never knowing where we were going to go, created a lot of stress for me. I felt squeezed on all sides.

I drew my energy from nature and horses. I breathed fresh air. I appreciated the joyful moments and being so close to my family (actually, we lived very, very closely together).

How could we have put ourselves in such a situation? The children themselves liked all these changes and it felt a bit like camping to them. They laughed and had fun. I loved feeling that my girls were happy.

We had a mountain of unopened boxes, and we functioned with the barest minimum. I, who always like my house to be tidy and clean, lived in places that I did not like at all.

We intensified our search for a home. Strangely, all of our offers were rejected for various reasons.

Finally, one evening in my room while I was alone, I questioned the Universe:

""Why are all our bids refused?"
"What is going to happen to us?"
"Where should we go?"

Then I declared what I no longer wanted. I did not want to have to move all the time for unknown periods. Then I clearly affirmed what I did want.

Nobody knew what I was asking the Universe for. I decided to ask in my own way, in my imaginary secret garden...

The next day, we got the inspiration to visit a new housing development to see if there was land for sale. The ideal plot was waiting for us. We immediately made an offer to purchase and everything was accepted. I was ecstatic.

A few days later, the plan of our future home was chosen. Sylvain dug the foundations and we contracted various specialists to construct the house. We put all our energy and heart into it. Several months later we moved into this new house. It was ready just in time because... once again, we had to leave the house we occupied temporarily, since it had been sold.

That is how the Universe delivers our desires. Never, never, would I have dreamed of having a new home like this.

As soon as I asked and stated clearly what I wanted, the Universe arranged everything for us. Everything was so easy. The Universe once again, delivered so much more than I had hoped for. I love this house. It is a gift from the Universe.

This example shows you how I asked the Universe. It is always so spontaneous. I speak and write with my heart, with my emotions. It is my secret garden.

If you wish, you can share your realization techniques once they have been manifested. However, you may encounter people who will be doubtful and this can make you doubt. These energies are contagious. Do not let anyone discourage you.

After all, you are the one who creates your life. You do not have to justify yourself...

☯ Recommended Actions

Make your requests to the
Universe spontaneously.
Keep them to yourself.
Create your own secret garden
with the requests that you
keep in your heart.

Chapter 33

Conclusion

*I*t's not the end, but the beginning of your new life!

You have assimilated a lot of very powerful information that has the power to transform your life. However you must make the decision to apply this information so that these wonderful changes can take place.

If you have taken action and put into practice the tools that inspire you, that make sense for your personality, it is clear that changes and victories are already appearing. It is the Law of Attraction which is always infallible. The Universe delivers what you focus your attention on.

Here are the steps that will transform your life:

1. Accept responsibility for the current conditions in your life. Stop being a victim and making others responsible for what you have attracted. You are the creator of your life. You attract your current life with your beliefs, your thoughts and your emotions. If your current life does not please you, you must make changes in your beliefs, your

thoughts and your emotions. To change your life, you must change your way of doing things and develop creative habits.

2. Decide what you want now and for your future. Be determined and persistent. Focus all your attention on your goals. These desires must awaken an intense passion in you.

3. Be positive and surround yourself with positive people. Be inspired by nature and find your way to draw continual energy from it.

4. Be grateful for all you have and all your small or large victories.

5. Take action continually. Repetition is the key to implementing sustainable change. Use the methods or tools that I have proposed to you throughout this book. Choose the ones that resonate with you.

6. Do what you love, what stimulates you.

7. Love yourself. Send out love and help others.

8. Use your victories, large or small to spur you on to reach bigger goals.

9. Enjoy nature every day. It is an oasis of energy.

10. Smile, because your life is being transformed in such a positive way.

YOU CAN DO IT !

If you decide today to change in a positive way, by even just a thought, a behavior, a habit, you're on the road to success and the achievement of a better life.

You can do it, because you are a Creator. You have the power to create the life of your dreams! You can be, have and do what you want, using your imagination and emotions. Your mind is the key that will give you the access to your dreams.

Your happiness is so close...

However, you will not find happiness in material things. Your happiness is within you! All you have to do is let it out and take flight like the chick who leaves the nest to enjoy life.

As for me, I have enjoyed sharing my story and my tools with you. If I have been able to inspire you to improve yourself and thereby improve your life, then I will be fulfilled. My dream has come true.

By changing one thought at a time, one person at a time, we all contribute to a better world for everyone.

To your present and future success!

I love you!

The Universe loves you too!

Bibliography

Some information in this book comes from various sources (books, Internet documents, and recordings). I propose some reading material to you that I have appreciated and which may inspire you. You can also refer to our websites for numerous tools to generate abundance and prosperity in your life:

www.abundancethrunature.com

Allen, James: As A Man Thinketh
Andrews, Andy: The Noticer
Audlin, Mindy: What If It All Goes Right?
Byrne, Rhonda: The Secret
Byrne, Rhonda: The Power
Canfield, Jack: Success According to Jack
Covey, Stephan R: The 7 Habits of Highly Effective People
Dyer, Dr Wayne: The Power of Intention
Eker, T Harv: Secrets of a Millionaire Mind
Forster, Sandy: How To Be Wildly Wealthy Fast
Haanel, Charles F.: The Master Key System
Hill, Napoléon: Think and Grow Rich
Morel, Marc-André: La Cinquième Saison
Murphy, Joseph: The Power of Your Subconscious Mind
Peck, Scott: Le Chemin le Moins Fréquenté
Ponder, Catherine: The Dynamic Laws of Prosperity
Proctor, Bob: High Self-esteem and Unshakable Confidence

Robin, Anthony: Unlimited Power
Shimoff, Marci: Happy For No Reason
Vitale, Joe: The Attractor Factor
Vitale, Joe: Zero Limits
Wattles, Wallace D.: The Science of Being Great

About the author

Sylvie Vallee was born in Ontario, but spent much of her childhood in Quebec, Canada. She is second in a family of three children. She lived the first years of her childhood on military bases, since her father was in the army.

When she was very young, she developed a love for nature, horses and dogs. This was reflected in her drawings. Rather solitary, Sylvie perfected her manual skills. She loves to create. In her spare time, she spends time alone in nature with her dog. She remains active in sports.

After her studies in Computer Science, she began her career as a IT (Information Technology) manager for the government. She rose through the ranks by developing her management, leadership and organizational skills. Spontaneously, people at her job, came talk to her about their problems and challenges. People amicably call her a psychologist. She listens to people and loves to help them find solutions. She understands that people like to feel listened to and supported.

She developed an interest in everything related to personal growth. During her spare time, she studies everything she can about this subject.

She works in Information technology (IT) project management. Her knowledge and experience will be the basis for real estate projects that she likes.

Very family oriented, Sylvie was married at age twenty-one. She experienced pregnancy eight times, with three miscarriages and five wonderful daughters. She adores children.

Wife, mother of five children, manager of numerous projects and entrepreneur, she organizes her time to be able to carry out her responsibilities and live with passion.

Her journey filled with challenges, allowed her to develop various talents and creative techniques. Love of nature stimulates her to make choices that transform her life.

With her husband, Sylvain and their five daughters, she runs a family business that stimulates passion. She develops training projects using horseback riding for children and for adults. The originality of the services offered delights everyone.

She devotes herself to what she is passionate about: family, personal growth, horses, nature and real estate. She is always learning and sharing her knowledge in a natural and fun way.

Her mind is always buzzing with projects. She loves life and her enthusiasm is contagious. She is inspired.

In her own way, she contributes to a better world by helping families improve their lives.

One thought at a time and one person at a time!

Sylvie is a dynamic, authentic and inspiring entrepreneur and author. She helps families understand how to enhance the way they think, speak, feel and vibrate so that they can attract all their dreams.

For information about the free materials, products and workshops of Sylvie Vallee that relate to your personal development, you can visit:

www.abundancethrunature.com

www.ingramcontent.com/pod-product-compliance
Lightning Source LLC
Chambersburg PA
CBHW071956090426
42740CB00011B/1961